Christianity:

The End of Spiritual Confusion

Transform Your Zeal for God into Knowledge of the Christ

by

Bishop Lloyd U. Nsek, Sr.

FolioAvenue Publishing Service
2031 Union Street, Suite 6,
San Francisco CA 94123
415-869-8834 (866-365-4628)
www.folioavenue.com

ISBN: 978-1-951193-72-0

FOLIO
AVENUE

TABLE OF CONTENTS

The Foreword

As a Bishop, called by the Lord Jesus Christ, according to the will of God the Father, this book is my clarion call to you who dwell on the face of the earth. I am not seeking to persuade you to join me to uphold and disseminate another religious or sectarian of moral behavior. I am however, calling you to take a second look at a philosophy essential to enabling us to be all that we long to be as people on the face of the earth. I am asking your uninterrupted and keen attention to the doctrine of Jesus Christ. I am asking you to revisit your Christian faith. I am asking you to revisit Christianity and catch what it truly represents.

Based on misinformation and lack of knowledge, believers and non-believers alike have put a label on Christianity. As a result, the world—its real and intended audience from the beginning— calls it a mere religion. On the one hand the practice of Christianity is skewed, away from its truth as the more practical guide for humanity. On the other hand, it is also skewed to the point people deny its power to be the final authority on bringing out the best in every man and woman.

Religions of this world fall short of this noble achievement. At their best, they prove to be the catalyst for contentions and endemic divisiveness in the world.

Rather than promote unity, religions have become ominous agents of polarization. In the name of God, religious laws coupled with sectarian ordinances have been imposed on a majority in the interest of a minority that live in total hypocrisy. This book calls these things out to the open view.

Jesus Christ broke religious laws and sectarian ordinances to initialize Christianity. For that, He died, being put to death by

i

religious leaders, but was resurrected on the third day as proof of the power in His words. This became a prime example that all mere religion really does is kill, but Christianity gives life. This is the core value of this book to you.

This book is written for you, who are most qualified to rip off the false label pinned on Christianity calling it an organized religion.

It is not. We must now separate the "Truth" from the "Lies" and forever be free.

When you study the life and teachings of Jesus Christ you will discover secrets that will make our planet a better place for humanity.

You will:

- Know much more about the chaos and upheavals we face in the world.

- Trace its roots

- Unravel the mystery that humans are not just flesh-and-blood beings

We are truly spirit beings on the inside.

Falsely practiced as a mere religion, Christians have missed out on the opportunity and honor of sharing with humanity the solution for its main human problem—**the spirit within a person**. Since Jesus broke religious laws when he established Christianity, His doctrine is not religious. This, in turn, makes Christianity not a mere religion, but the philosophy of life in general.

No wonder He gave us these catch phrases: "…for God so loved the world; … go ye into all nations; … He died for the sin of the whole world; … and you shall be my witnesses in Jerusalem; … go to Judea and Samaria and to the ends of the earth."

Dedication

I have the honor of dedicating this book to the Lord Jesus Christ. He is the one who planted the seed in me all these years that has yielded the fruit we now hold, open and read.

By His grace, I found my lovely wife, Minister Josephine Nsek, who has been a pillar of His mercies and love in my life. Together, we have been blessed with three wonderful children and a step-son. These are their names: Estee Nsek—UCLA graduate, Lloyd Jr. Nsek—still in the University, Magdalene Nsek—still in High School, and Seuti Kamara—my step son, who has given us the lovely Dasani and the lovely Brooklyn as grandchildren. My special dedication goes out to my wonderful parents: Engr.,& Mrs. Nsek, and my in-laws: the late Mr. Akosi and Madame Nwane Akininalapikia. Also, Belema Debra Ogulu, a cousin with an unwavering hope. And you, Mr. Ed Winsor Wright; time has finally spoken that we are just like family.

I would be remiss if I failed to personally dedicate this book to the numerous ministries, churches and fellowships that were pivotal to our growth and development through the years in Christianity. My God shall supply all your needs.

I must extend a heartfelt dedication to the late Jack Mock. He was my dear friend and a prophet. He lives now in loving memory in my heart. How can I forget Pastor Verne Hatfield? He was the one who ordained us into the gospel. God spoke through him to us about the future of America and the world. In 1994 he was the one who prophesied about the coming into office of President Barak Obama, the first Black President in America. We love you Hatfield. Hello to you, Pastor Andre Wilson. I miss you personally.

This is to you Pastors Gil and Sharon Prichard, Pastors Roy and

Judith Young, Pastor Don Hunter and the entire Water of Life Community Church family.

Finally, I'd like to humbly dedicate this book to these good people with whom I share a personal connection: Dr. Francis & Gloria Nyong—for being there at the critical turning point in my life. Mr. Gabriel & Josephine Odudu, I thank you for love so strong and then some. Also, Olusola Oyemade, MD., Jesse & Frankie Fitchett, Mrs. Ruth Collins, Mr. & Mrs. Charles Sudderth, Mr. Anthony Orimolade, Mr. & Mrs. Imeh AkpanUdosen, Lena V. Hamilton, Engr. Francis Akpan Okon, Pastor Joseph & Ekaette Iton, Mr. Julius Ephraim, Mr. Ufot Andrew NkpoIdet, Bruce Russell, Fatmatta Hallussein, Mr. Wilfred Essien, Michael & Ikwo Archibong, Patrick & Catherine Ekanem, Iffiok & Angie Nsek, and Stanley Etuk.

I dedicate this book to all of you for your long suffering and patience. You have allowed the will of God to be perfected in me seeking His kingdom through these years. It's true: His kingdom comes first and His righteousness then the Sapphire project we pursued prior can be added. You all were never forgotten. My tears are wiped off now.

With much gratitude, I end this dedication with a vote of thanks to Antonia Essien, Esq., Ena Rideau, Ngozi Nwosu, Thomas Figuracion, Engr. Fakumo & Tariere Dick, Mr. Kabowei & Felicia Akamande, Mr. & Mrs. Joshua Adegbe, Mr. & Mrs. Wilson Akinmulero, Dele & Esther Silva, and Fidel & Rose Ozuna. Your names are in the Lamb's Book of Life.

The Unseen Veil of the Christian Apostasy

Have you ever held onto a belief so long and thought you were right only to find out that you were all wrong?

It was not easy for me after having been taught nearly 40 years of Christian doctrine, which I'd observed since I was a child, to let that go and start all over again. Undergoing that change to take hold of the core beliefs of Christianity felt like I was sitting on top of the swinging pendulum ball of faith. It swung from Christianity-according-to-my-church-and-myself, on the left, to the Christianity-according-to-Christ Jesus, Himself, on the right.

Most Christians I know find it hard to believe there are diametrically opposed, philosophical differences within the nominal church. As a result, anytime I mentioned this idea in conversations with friends, the atmosphere in the room would change. Everything and everyone's demeanor would become altered like the two Alka Seltzer tablets dropped into a glass of water. The conversation almost always ended in a heated and spirited argument.

Let's face it. Friends can argue from time to time. But when such arguments turn to acts of hatred between friends, then it certainly begs the question: What is wrong here? Initially, I could not understand, for the life of me, why anyone who bears the name of Christ and is called a Christian, claiming to follow Him, would refuse to embrace what Jesus Christ personally does, speaks, and says He is.

This is the thin, fine line that I have seen all these years proving to be elusive and hard to detect by Christians all over the world. This may have happened because people have been doing what they generally observed their fellow Christians do instead of taking the time to probe the scriptures for themselves. I bet my bottom dollar that anyone who takes the time to search the scriptures will discover the difference between what Jesus says and does and what his followers routinely say and do.

Searching the scriptures faithfully will tear down this artificial wall of ignorance and trample it under our feet.

It is time to stop making excuses for not spending the necessary time in studying the Word of God. We should now stop and take full notice of it as an extraordinary phenomenon indeed—the God of the universe speaks to us and we don't take time to find out for ourselves what he is saying.

We need not blame our Pastors, Teachers, Evangelists and Preachers for it, but only ourselves. There is not enough blame that we can emotionally and psychologically pin on our 21st century world and busy lifestyles to successfully absolve ourselves of the simple responsibility of reading up on the physical person of Jesus Christ in the Bible.

If we were to individually take the time to meticulously and judiciously study the person of Jesus Christ, then you and I would really see it. Indeed, we would see the thin, fine line that separates Jesus Christ according to the Jewish religious sects (Pharisees, Sadducees, and Scribes) versus Jesus Christ, Son of the living God, who epitomizes all that is good and perfect about our humanity.

This is the point of grave and egregious misconception in relation to Jesus Christ that has remained to this day. Many are under the belief that since He was born a Jew, He came to pick up from where Moses stopped. In essence, He would join the Jewish religious sects to maintain the traditions of the elders and of the temple. In doing so, Jesus Christ would be seen going around collecting tithes and offerings for temple upkeep according to the Law. Also, He would never say anything in contrast or in opposition to the writings of Moses and the Prophets of Israel.

That is where they all went wrong about Jesus Christ the real Son of the living God. He never paid tithes for temple upkeep. He never collected tithes from the people even though He spent considerable amounts of time teaching, healing and feeding them real foods. He certainly did not offer animals in the temple for His sins in accordance with the Jewish law of atonement. Instead, He fought against the money-changers in the temple advocating piety for the house of God.

As an observer, something here begins to click in my mind about the Bible in relation to God's key messengers over the generations gone by. I observe that they all had a unique and different mission synchronized for their respective times and places on the earth:

- God gave Adam instruction on the tree in the midst of the garden. He and Eve were not to eat of the fruit from that tree of the knowledge of good and evil.

- God assigned Noah to build the Ark.

- God promised Abraham that he would have a son after he had grown too old, along with his wife Sarah, to bear children. From that promise, God brought forth the nation of Israel.

- God gave Moses him the Law so that Israel can now be conscious of sin in the world.

- God made Jesus Christ the end-game plan—the one to wrap things up for humanity in this present world bringing us, sin-free, into the new world prepared anew by God, called the kingdom of God and the new Jerusalem, which has been revealed to be coming down from heaven unto this earth soon.

Of course, His assignment is apt to be distinctly different from all others, especially from that of Moses. So why do we not hold this thought in our Christian minds?

To every Christian, it should be a well-known fact that Jesus is not following after Moses and the prophets in the Old Testament. Rather, they all were trying to follow after Jesus, but without the accuracy of doctrine.

Such accurate doctrine of Jesus was not yet written since it had to be written by Him and Him alone in the physical flesh of His appearing by virtue of His spoken words. Those words, I might add here, Jesus says are not like normal human words that we speak to one another every day. But as Jesus divinely explains: "the words I speak to you they are spirit and they are life" (John 6:63).

Right there, my friend, the difference is clear. No one else throughout the Bible was ever that bold. That means Jesus Christ has something superior to all others in the Bible who came before Him. In addition, He says all that He is and possesses is available to us if we believe in Him. Therefore, we should ask, seek and knock for all He is and possesses.

As a result, we are to be like the person the Lord Jesus is in the gospel. But this is the caveat: it will take His spoken words that came out of His own mouth physically in the flesh to transform us, who now live in our human flesh.

Here is finally the divine mystery behind the words spoken by Jesus, the difference between His words and those spoken by the likes of Isaiah, Jeremiah, Ezekiel, Malachi, and the rest of the Old Testament prophets: it is our heavenly Father Himself, the supreme God of the entire universe, speaking from within His own Son to us—according to John 12:44-50.

> [44] Jesus cried and said, He that believeth on me, believeth not on me, but on him that sent me.
>
> [45] And he that seeth me seeth him that sent me.
>
> [46] I am come a light into the world, that whosoever believeth on me should not abide in darkness.
>
> [47] And if any man hear my words, and believe not, I judge him not: for I came not to judge the world, but to save the world.
>
> [48] He that rejecteth me, and receiveth not my words, hath one that judgeth him: the word that I have spoken, the same shall judge him in the last day.
>
> [49] For I have not spoken of myself; but the Father, which sent me, he gave me a commandment, what I should say, and what I should speak.
>
> [50] And I know that his commandment is life everlasting: whatsoever I speak therefore, even as the Father said unto me, so I speak.

This was not true for the Old Testament Prophets. As for all of them, from Prophet Samuel to Malachi, the gospel reveals that these ones received and spoke those words in the Bible by the "direction of angels"—according to Acts 7:51-53.

[51] Ye stiff-necked and uncircumcised in heart and ears, ye do always resist the Holy Ghost: as your fathers did, so do ye.

[52] Which of the prophets have not your fathers persecuted? and they have slain them which shewed before of the coming of the Just One; of whom ye have been now the betrayers and murderers:

[53] Who have received the law by the disposition of angels, and have not kept it.

They did not have what Jesus Christ had according to Colossians 2:9.

[9] For in him dwelleth all the fulness of the Godhead bodily.

Simply put, as our heavenly Father has the sovereignty to decide to wrap things up with mankind in order to usher in a better world than this present wicked one, He stopped sending angels out to meet with humans. Rather, He comes by Himself through His Son to us. This is indeed in agreement with Genesis 1:26.

[26] And God said, Let us make man in our image, after our likeness: and let them have dominion over the fish of the sea, and over the fowl of the air, and over the cattle, and over all the earth, and over every creeping thing that creepeth upon the earth.

Except in the New Testament, it is as if you could hear the Godhead saying "let us go and save man from Satan and the demons and bring man into life with us and make him like us."

Since God is a Spirit, everything about Him and from Him is

Spirit. Remember we are to be like Him. He is not like us. That is the journey and the final destination for us humans. That is why His spoken words to us in these last days by His Son are "spirit and life." For the simple truth that we are made in His image and likeness, He couldn't have come for us by an angel anymore. Angels are not made in His image and likeness. **Only we humans do completely compliment God in all things.** He needed a human body for the sake of truth and compatibility.

As a result, He planted His seed, Christ, in the womb of a human virgin in Israel named Mary. There, He made that holy seed in Mary His dwelling place in order to educate, consecrate and sanctify humanity.

That is why Jesus Christ says, "If you have seen me you have seen the Father" (John 14:7). That is why the gospel reveals that Jesus took this message to those left in hell since the days of Noah to the time of the crucifixion so that they too might believe in Jesus Christ and be saved just like the living. In appearing to them in hell, Jesus did not, I repeat, did not bring them words spoken by any Prophet of the Old Testament like we in the church are preaching about in these last days.

Those words lack the ingredient to deliver, let alone save mankind. The reason for that is hereby revealed: those words were witnessed to by archangels and ratified using the blood of earthly animals.

These were just shadows pending the real thing, whereas, the spoken word by Jesus Christ to us comes witnessed to by the Father Himself and ratified on earth using the super-precious blood of Jesus. Hence, the old lacked the power to transform mankind.

No wonder people were always stoned to death instead of being given a tiny chance for repentance and deliverance. In our natural growth process, if we venture out and eat non-nutritious foods for our human body, then we consequently deprive ourselves of excellent health. We become sickly, instead of vibrant. Our overall skin tone and luster becomes dull and not glowing. In turn, we simply grow weak and die. But people dread the thought of death knocking on their doors.

We already have the intelligence to avoid knowingly poisoning ourselves in the natural. We know not to ingest things dangerous to our health.

Let us apply the same principle with respect to the Bible scriptures. They represent our spiritual food for our spiritual growth. When we eat the Old Testament spiritual food, we remain weak and sickly spiritually. But when we eat the New Testament spiritual food, we have power over witchcraft and such evil things of this life and of this present world.

Every cursed thing we inherited from our ancestors, who were themselves pagans are indeed cleansed from our bloodline. Jesus Christ remains the epitome of the Word of God with such better ingredients for mankind. Do you get it now? He is our spiritual food for life. Everything in Him comes fresh and potent for us. That is why He stipulated that "…you are already clean because of the words which I have spoken to you" (John 15:3).

But if you do not read and abide in the spoken words of Christ by Christ, how will you get this great benefit? Further, to prove how indispensable His spoken words are to this present age, He says all humanity is going to be judged on the account of these words (John 12:48).

Do you know what this means? None of us will be asked by our heavenly Father about what the Prophet Isaiah said. Nor will God ask anyone of us about what King Solomon said and wrote in the book of Proverbs.

Maybe we think that we will regurgitate the Psalms or the Ecclesiastes to Him on that day. Perhaps, the writings of Moses as well as any Prophet of the Old Testament will suffice when we stand before God the Father. To that end, Jesus Christ made it clear what that distinction is and the separation of the two Testaments again.

> [36] And he spake also a parable unto them; No man putteth a piece of a new garment upon an old; if otherwise, then both the new maketh a rent, and the piece that was taken out of the new agreeth not with the old.
>
> [37] And no man putteth new wine into old bottles; else the new wine will burst the bottles, and be spilled, and the bottles shall perish.
>
> [38] But new wine must be put into new bottles; and both are preserved.
>
> [39] No man also having drunk old wine straightway desireth new: for he saith, 'The old is better.'"
>
> (Luke 5:36-39).

Given the clarity of the distinction of the two books of the Testaments, one is apt to ask why they are lumped together in the Bible. Certainly, it was not done to bring about confusion. God is not the author of confusion as the gospel reveals to us.

Therefore, the reason they are lumped together in the Bible is for the purpose of audit and accountability of God's relentless outreach to humanity from age to age without fail or exhaustion. It tells us, alongside human characters, what and how God kept molding humanity in readiness for this last age.

Now that we are here in the last days of this age, He brings in the missing piece of the puzzle—His Son in human flesh.

In setting the valuation of the gospel to us all, Jesus minced no words as He said the God whom we all seek has now offered His holy, personal and direct involvement in it. That is why it is of more value than anything else in the Bible. In the Old, He merely sent out angels to visit with mankind on His behalf.

But why is He opting to be personally involved now? God sincerely craves an intimate relationship with us humans He created to be like Him. That is the remarkable difference with respect to the gospel in comparison. It is indeed the thing Jesus says in Matthew 13:16-17, all the Prophets of Old desired to see, but did not. Now see how special and fortunate we are in these last days. Let's take full advantage of this my friends.

Examine Your Christianity

So the questions we ought to ask ourselves about our Christianity are these:

(1) Is my Christianity according to my church and Pastor (Non-Transformational message), or is my Christianity according to Jesus Christ (Transformational message)?

(2) There is no confusion as to the difference given the warning of Jesus in Luke 5:36-39. I would be remiss if I failed to add that there is more than one warning message in the gospel like that one in the book of Luke.

(3) Therefore, we ought to always be on the alert. We ought to always catch ourselves or others who might inadvertently err.

Let me explain the Christianity according to Jesus Christ for our understanding.

First, it is centered on the life and works of the person of Jesus Christ. It accounts for His earthly time from His earthly birth, like yours and mine, out of the womb of the Virgin Mary to His resurrection from the dead and ascension into heaven physically.

It serves to enable us to draw a close-knit identity with Him on all human levels and every human experience of today's life. We see Him like us and us like Him. We begin to see Him in our everyday situations and circumstances, no matter how crazy or stupid they might be.

We must now remember that Jesus Christ lived life as a human also. Therefore, if we humans like to drink whatever we are into drinking, He also drank. Plus, He totally understands how a human can crave for booze and such human things. He therefore can deliver you from going overboard like we sometimes do.

Jesus was able to strike a perfect balance in His humanity like no one else ever could since the creation of man. He was successful by reason of having the right Spirit inside His human body—the Spirit of our heavenly Father. This indeed is the bread and butter of Christianity for you and I.

Our heavenly Father is intentionally on the move to put His Spirit inside you and I. To demonstrate that to us, He put His Son out to break the shackles of sins and death and get us cleaned up for life.

Replace Scriptures of the Old in your Heart with the New

We cannot be made clean if we neglect the person of Jesus and embrace the Prophets of Old like we do in our churches today. To become clean, we must first of all understand what is being cleansed and the role of the Law of Moses in our lives.

The role of the Law was to expose sin that was always present in the world since the day of the fall of man in the garden. In exposing it, the writ of the Law called sin out by its individual names to our knowledge. After doing that, the Law rested and did nothing more about sin except condemn us for it.

For you and I in this world, the names of sin are not just labels attached to unscrupulous human behaviors. By and large, they are the actual foul and unclean spirits living inside of us every day we live our lives. For example, sins of fornication, adultery, malice, gossip, back biting, hate, corruption, bribery, and so forth are unclean spirits living inside of us. Therefore, when they manifest in us through our behaviors, it is a revelation to us of our intimate relationship we have maintained with these demons.

Jesus Christ, upon being here in this present world physically, had the task of casting out these demons from people. As a result, they were clean. With His twelve disciples, He made the people clean by giving them the gospel Word of God. As the gospel Word of God penetrated the hearts, souls and minds of the disciples, these demons fled from within and were cast out. That was why Judas remained clean until the hour of the betrayal of Jesus after the last supper. The Bible tells us that in order for Judas to betray Jesus, Satan entered into him (Luke 22:3). Judas did not do it all on his own accord.

Since Jesus is now at the right hand of God in heaven, He left us the same gospel Word of God that kept His disciples clean and demon-free on the inside.

In essence, that is the role of the gospel Word of God in our lives. To become clean, we must diligently search and find replacement "word" in the New Testament for those scriptures of Old. For example, if you are in the habit of quoting the following scripture: "...my people perish from lack of knowledge," then instinctively replace it with a life-giving "word" such as, "...but we have the mind of Christ." (1 Corinthians 2:16).

That means whatever once may have seemed insurmountable, you have now positioned yourself to face it head on.

Second, the word tells you this: "...but the anointing which you have received from Him abides in you, and you do not need that anyone teach you, but as the same anointing teaches you concerning all things, and is true, and is not a lie, and just as it has taught you, you will abide in Him" (1 John 2:27).

Also, you are well able to empower others by your knowledge of the Christ in you. Now with that replacement word, you get the sense that things are not hopeless around you. Since Christ is an all-knowing personality, by identifying with Him, fear is immediately pushed out of your mind.

But wait, let me ask you this: do you know exactly where to look up each of the replacement words above in the Bible? If you do, then bless your heart. If you don't, then it is time to examine your Christianity. Such divine knowledge should have already been in you by now. This discovery serves as the spiritual indicator telling you that you do not have the extra oil in your lamp.

25 Then shall the kingdom of heaven be likened unto ten virgins, which took their lamps, and went forth to meet the bridegroom. ² And five of them were wise, and

five were foolish. ³ They that were foolish took their lamps, and took no oil with them: ⁴ But the wise took oil in their vessels with their lamps. ⁵ While the bridegroom tarried, they all slumbered and slept. ⁶ And at midnight there was a cry made, Behold, the bridegroom cometh; go ye out to meet him. ⁷ Then all those virgins arose, and trimmed their lamps. ⁸ And the foolish said unto the wise, Give us of your oil; for our lamps are gone out. ⁹ But the wise answered, saying, Not so; lest there be not enough for us and you: but go ye rather to them that sell, and buy for yourselves. ¹⁰ And while they went to buy, the bridegroom came; and they that were ready went in with him to the marriage: and the door was shut. ¹¹ Afterward came also the other virgins, saying, Lord, Lord, open to us. ¹² But he answered and said, Verily I say unto you, I know you not. ¹³ Watch therefore, for ye know neither the day nor the hour wherein the Son of man cometh. (Matt. 25:1-13).

Make this time count for you to put the extra oil of the Word of God in your lamps.

Here is another popular saying amongst us: "…no weapon formed against you shall prosper and every tongue rising up against you in judgment, you shall condemn" (Isaiah 54:17**).** Now, ask yourself: what word in Christ Jesus should replace this one in your time of prayer? How about this word: "…behold I give you authority to tread on scorpions and serpents and over all the power of the enemy, nothing shall by no means hurt you" (Luke 10:19). I think you get the kingdom idea now.

If we all engage in this spiritual exercise, we will experience a complete makeover in no time. Our Christian mind will be totally renewed. We would now have that 'mustard-seed faith'

Jesus talked about. We would be well-able to literally move mountains and do the greater works He said we would do, which we have not yet done.

Seeing just how far I have come in Christ and all the breaking of strongholds that His word in me has produced, it is absolutely worth it for me and my family to escape the rut that we were in prior to discovering the unseen veil of the Christian apostasy. Let me share with you my personal story below.

I was just 12 years old when I gave my life to the Lord Jesus Christ. It was not something I planned to do in 1974 that awesome day in Calabar, formally South Eastern State of Nigeria.

Today, the country has undergone huge transformation with particular emphasis on creating more states. As a result, Calabar is now more geographically positioned within the nucleus of its tribal folks. Consequently, my family and a huge majority of my tribal folks have now relocated to our own state, rightly named Akwa Ibom State.

Before this exodus occurred, my family lived in one of the good parts of Calabar. When I say good part, I mean one of the areas in Calabar with good housing built with cement and bricks. There was a pipe-borne-water supply and good plumbing system, and the level of comfort was highly appreciated given the living standards of that time. You could say we were considered belonging to the middle class. With that in mind, all we did as a family of six was the obvious: parents working, children attending school, and everybody going to church on Sunday.

We were and still are members of the Apostolic Church. Our

church family was rather large. There was strong faith in God—at least to my understanding as a youngster. I witnessed a strong move of the Holy Spirit. Devout men and women of faith used their spiritual gifts to bless others. Some were prophesied to, and those things came to pass. Some received healing of the mind. Some received healing for all the various ailments that plagued them.

I still remember vividly a man who was brought in during that time. He was in his late twenties and afflicted with insanity. The elders of the church made a place for him to sleep on the side veranda of the church. From time to time, he would mutter things or mumble words while wagging his index finger in the air.

Since this was his condition, no one looked at him as being weird even though he really was. It took some period of time before his miracle healing happened. But all through what seemed like forever actually became a ninety-day season of waiting upon the Lord Jesus Christ. Then suddenly, this young man was restored completely to normalcy. I watched this with my own eyes as a kid. I was taken by that miracle of God. As good as that might sound to you here, I must let you know that it was just the beginning, and I was still in elementary school.

Just before starting high school, I auditioned and got accepted into the church choir and sang alto. The choir Master was a nice person overall. In today's comparison checklist, he would pass for Blair Underwood, the Hollywood actor. He was of average height with a dark chocolate luster of skin tone. Oh yes, he knew how to conduct song services. Even to this day, some of those songs still stream through the portals of my mind from time to time. I must tell you that they pick me up when I am feeling down.

I felt led to join the intercessory prayer team after my good friend, Asuquo, surprised me and the rest of our clique of youngsters with the gift of prophesy during one of the full-church evening services. As the Pastor brought the congregation to a moment of silence after song worship and supplications, like a lightening rod, we all heard his voice ring out with prophecy for the whole church. Asuquo spoke with clarity in his voice and the tone was equally persuasive, indeed. Given the large capacity and the crowd that night at the church, no ten-year-old boy would dare try such a thing even as a mere prank. The deacon on duty rushed the microphone close to this young prophet while he spoke as the Holy Spirit gave him utterance. Since his voice was amplified by the microphone, he sounded like an angel speaking from heaven with the peculiar pitch of innocence often associated with a typical ten-year-old boy. Let me tell you, it carried with it such an indescribable purity falling in my ears.

As mesmerized as I was, I told myself I must follow the steps as Asuquo and the rest of the intercessory prayer team and be used of God. Being now a full-fledged member, I was careful not to miss participating in the regular Friday-night prayer vigil. This activity truly opened me up to the deeper concepts of faith and spirituality; at least, so I thought.

For starters, I would join the group and indulge in the reading of scriptures from the Old Testament. The favorite ones came from the book of Psalms. Everyone would engage in spiritual warfare exercise. There was something about the writ of the Psalms that spoke too well for the people with respect to their issues and circumstances. Therefore we all adapted to the language and the emotional vernacular of the Psalms in order to be victorious through prayer.

I became an eyewitness observer to the numerous accounts of victory over witchcraft curses and spells that were placed upon people to mess up their lives by the wicked folks with whom they came in contact. I saw people get delivered from the wicked manipulations of voodoo activity staged by local medicine men and women in the greater community against the well-being of the victims.

On one occasion, I saw one of the deacons of the church leap up from his post during prayer and made his way to the Senior Pastor's house. The house was adjacent to the church building within the premises of the church grounds. The deacon, who was a male figure, went inside the Senior Pastor's house and came out with an axe. He then proceeded to the frontage of the Senior Pastor's house and began cutting the cement concrete directly in front of the main entry door of the house.

When he had succeeded in cracking the concrete open, he now used a shovel to dig through the ground like someone excavating for some hidden treasure. He was not adopting the usual carefulness in his attempt to exhume the treasure that is characteristic of archeologists. Instead, the deacon was panting and aggressive as he drove the shovel up and down in the ground removing the dirt beneath to quickly get to the hidden treasure.

After what seemed like a good ten minutes of manly workout and sweat, we heard a little noise ring out following the collision of the shovel head and a buried wooden doll. At this time, the deacon stopped digging. He placed his hand gently in the direction of the wooden doll and carefully removed it from the gaping hole he had created.

When he put it down to the ground as if to rest a little from all that digging he'd just completed, something beyond logic happened: the wooden doll raised its head from the ground and started to run on its two wooden feet from us. This was amazing to us. In that split moment of scare and frenzy, the deacon reached out his right hand and grabbed the wooden doll so that it would not escape from our sight. He ordered a bon fire to be made. When it was fanned to full and consuming flame, he threw the wooden doll into the flaming fire with everyone standing around encircling it.

After the doll had been a few seconds in the fire, a tiny, high-pitched voice rang out from the wooden doll just as if it did not want to remain there. Just as we all suspected, the wooden doll suddenly leaped out of the fire making its way of escape between the legs of the person immediately in front of it. In hindsight now I realize, no human fire was going to stop the wooden doll from carrying out its mission. The target as well as the object of its evil mission was the head Pastor of the Apostolic Church branch where it was sent.

But in the end, the deacon quickly picked up the wooden doll and did something to squash its escape plans. Before our own eyes, the deacon placed the wooden doll between his feet on the ground and axed it in two halves of equal parts. These two pieces of the wooden doll were thrown into the fire. We all stood around and watched it burn to ashes. There victory for everyone concerned.

My Personal Ignorance Regarding the Miracles, Signs, and Wonders

Growing up in that church in Calabar, I used to think that men and women like the deacon in the story above were invincible individuals. For all it's worth, I saw him as the hands and mouth of God to the flock. Look at how he was able to pinpoint the location of the hidden voodoo wooden doll buried under the Senior Pastor's frontage. Look at how he was able to exhume the doll and destroy it in the fire after prayer. For him to possess such power is nothing short of uncanny.

But when I took a closer look at his personal life and lifestyle, he really did not have it together considering the anointing I saw in him. It just seemed as though God worked well using him to deliver others. But as for him, the deacon, no such good report could be spoken of.

He had serious, personal issues that should have not lingered in his life given how powerfully he functioned in the church. This question loomed in my head for years. As I grew up and travelled to other places, this question in my head turned into a phenomenon to observe. I saw men and women of God who could move in their gifts of the Holy Spirit for the benefit of others, but lack joy in their personal lives. This lack of joy stems from them carrying sickness in their own bodies when they should be walking in healing all the time. Or, they have anger, temper, sexual and relational issues that prove hard to cure in their lives.

So what is really the problem here, I asked myself? Are they not anointed men and women of God? How is it that God will use them for others to get a word of prophecy, but leave them out in the cold? I have just too many questions to grapple with alone. Therefore, I went into prayer. God, in answering the prayer, took me to two significant individuals in the entire Christian Bible, to help me understand human nature. They are as follows: (1) the First Anointed Adam, and (2) the Second Anointed Adam, respectively. As the revelation kept pouring in from the Holy Spirit to me, everything made perfect sense.

By paying close attention to the Holy Spirit with regards to the two Adams in the Bible, I was able to unravel the hidden mystery about them and their effect on us humans. God, as it stands, was never to blame for anything affecting any human person born of a woman into this world. There is in fact no religion ever conjured or secular scholastic brilliance of man in the world today that has the capacity to shine this much light on this matter. It comes not by intellect, but by revelation only.

Accordingly, each Adam serves as a perimeter of God's boundary in His dealings with human affairs preceding the ushering in of the kingdom of God. In that respect, I found out that the First Adam was set at the starting point of humanity, whereas the Second Adam is at the finish line. The rest of us humans in the world are meticulously and purposefully sandwiched between the two Adams.

Each Adam was heavily anointed to function in his role in life. However, the anointing of each one has more weight in comparison to any other prophet or human who exists between them. The weight of their respective anointing is strictly in the capacity of an underwriter. Meaning, just like in real estate transactions, their underwriting anointing is what seals the deal for everyone coming through this present life. It is the underwriter that actually matches anyone, who is in the market to purchase a car or a house with the banks. It is the underwriter, who works out the terms of the loan as well as the monthly payments including the interest rates with the right banks. Such realistic decisions can never be made by all others, who are regular sales people.

In the final analysis, the home loan comes down from the underwriter in charge of the loan package and not the salesperson talking to us. We rarely meet with or know the underwriter.

Likewise, as a consequence of the fall of man, the anointing of the First Adam serves as a covering, with punitive intentions, over humanity until the time of the Second Adam—Jesus Christ—in this physical world. No human being on the face of the earth could escape its punitive grip on life. Not even Jesus Christ could escape death on the account of that anointing, even though He asked the Father for a possible escape, as Christians would recall, during the agonizing prayer in the garden of Gethsemane.

However, His death put an end to that anointing. To up the ante, Jesus rose from death and came back into the same human body he died in. It would interest you to know that the resurrection of Jesus Christ marks the beginning of the new anointing that serves as a covering without punitive intentions over humanity. Essentially, Jesus Christ, by coming into this world renders that first anointing expired.

But what did the expired anointing contain for the curious minds amongst us? It contained every word of God spoken and written for us humans from the First Adam up to the day of the birth of Jesus Christ—the Second Adam. For the reason of their expiration, Christians can no longer store them in their hearts, souls and minds. These expired scriptures prevent the Spirit that raised up Jesus from the dead from giving life to our mortal bodies.

Instead, we rob ourselves of healing, joy and power. Further, the evil spirits already living inside of us, except when we abide in the doctrine of Christ, still maintain their dominion over us. They are the agents of death in us without the Holy Spirit. It would interest you to know also that the Holy Spirit cannot come inside of us, being the promise of the Father, except you and I have the words of Jesus Christ abiding in us. He is sent to the earth to seal the new underwriting plan of God for us humans— eternal life. This life is in the Second Adam and is strictly and unequivocally derived from the spoken and revealed Word of the New Testament.

The Number One Mistake to Avoid

We must avoid maintaining the viewpoint that Christianity is practiced and produced from reading all the scriptures of the entire Bible. If it were true, then II Corinthians 3:13-15 would not have been written to the contrary.

> [13] And not as Moses, which put a veil over his face, that the children of Israel could not steadfastly look to the end of that which is abolished:
>
> [14] But their minds were blinded: for until this day remaineth the same veil untaken away in the reading of the Old Testament; which veil is done away in Christ.
>
> [15] But even unto this day, when Moses is read, the veil is upon their heart (II Corinthians 3:13-15).

Conversely, it would have completely stood behind such a view point and outright endorsed it. Instead, it totally forbids everybody; both Jew and Gentile, from reading and practicing Christianity save for one having a thorough knowledge of and building a personal relationship with Jesus Christ our Lord.

Therefore, we are not to be confused when we come across reference scriptures imported from the Old Testament and inserted in with the New Testament writings. It is indeed not a validation for us Gentiles (saved by His grace) to get back into reading of the Old Testament. Rather, it is done purely for the purpose of reiterating the fact that the Messiah the Jews were waiting for and expecting, is in fact this same Jesus Christ, whom the Gentiles are now worshipping.

In essence, it is meant to beckon our beloved non-Christian Jews to stop their endless search for the Messiah. He has already come as our Lord Jesus Christ in the human flesh. To that end, it is a clarion call for both Jews and Gentiles to meld into oneness in Christ the Messiah and be complete in Him. Hence, there is no other Messiah but Jesus Christ for all to worship and connect with God.

Now that we have been properly taught the truth about Christianity, it serves us best to take much heed and remain much centered in Christ. We do so by virtue of His word, which He spoke to both His disciples and the Jews in Jerusalem while being here on the earth two thousand years ago in the flesh.

As we can carefully observe, the Apostle Paul, once a Pharisee, gave up his belief in God by the **writ** of the Old Testament in order to gain Christ. When he converted from Judaism to Christianity, he sent out a stern warning that if anyone comes and preaches another gospel to you and I, let such a person be accursed. It is that serious, my dear Christian friend.

Do you think the Apostle Paul was just too extreme with that warning to us believers? No, I think not. We can begin to fathom it by drawing our attention to the issue of the warning labels placed on prescription drugs that we take to get well. Whether we purchase them over the counter or get them filled at the pharmacy, each drug is given an expiration date by the manufacturer. Once the drugs reach the expiration date on the label, the manufacturer fully expects us to throw them away and not use them again. We religiously throw those expired drugs away in the trashcan.

But what happens if we do not follow that instruction? We will learn the hard way that the same drugs that once saved us from sickness and diseases now, because of the expiration power, if ingested, turn into poison in our guts. We can actually die from them. Again, it matters not to the drugs that have expired if we knowingly or unknowingly swallowed them. Therefore, the blame is not shifted to the expired drugs for its wrongful use, but to the human user in question. That would be you and I.

Apparently, in the days of Apostle Paul, there were others, who came around mixing the Old Testament with the New Testament. Therefore, he gave that warning. In doing so, he was right in step with our Lord Jesus, who also gave a ground breaking warning to the Jewish people while the Apostle Paul was still a Pharisee under the name of Saul of Tarsus. According to Jesus, in Matthew 15:8, it is herein paraphrased to explain to us that there is an imminent danger of worshipping God in vain.

> This people draweth nigh unto me with their mouth, and honoureth me with their lips; but their heart is far from me
> (Matthew 15:8).

Meaning, when we falsely practice our Christianity not according to Jesus Christ, we have no connection with God whatsoever. We might be deceived into thinking we do when in actuality, we do not. In other words, God cannot, on account of His Son, accept from any one of us prayers and worship that jumps right out of the Old Testament writings. To do that would make God a liar.

It is written that truth and grace came by Jesus Christ. The Law of Moses was not the truth, but merely facts of our human lives. Truth is much bigger than the facts in the sense that it reveals what is behind the human facts. It is a fact that we get angry, argue, fight, hate and even kill one another. But the truth reveals that we do not do these evil things solely by our human will. There is a foul and unclean spirit behind our evil acts.

For the sake of truth, God wants to clean us up before bringing us into His face-to-face presence. He wants to remove the spiritual veil separating us from Him in this age the same way He tore in twain the physical veil in the Temple in Jerusalem while Jesus was on the cross at Calvary.

The thing we must realize is that the temple in Jerusalem closely mirrors the state of our soul with God. As the veil covered the Holy of Holies, where the most sacred things were carried out and transacted with God, so does an invisible veil lay across our hearts—the presence of demons in us.

We may recall Jesus saying that out of the heart flows the issues of this life. The ancient genealogies and traditions of the Israelites and so forth cannot tear down the veil embedded within us with evil nature. Since mankind was created in the image and the likeness of God, then it is only fair that God gives us all that we need to prove that fact about our lives to the rest of creation in the greater universe.

From the standpoint of the created that depends totally on the Creator, it is therefore God's sole burden to help position us to conform to His righteous and ever-loving nature, if He finds us falling short. Thanks to our God almighty, He has satisfied that burden for us all by giving us His Son Jesus Christ. Along with Jesus, God gave us life-giving word for our veiled souls. Those are the words Jesus spoke to the disciples and the Jewish nation. Taken together, those words constitute the Gospel. When we abide in those words, the veil is torn down from our souls and our hearts. In turn, it becomes easy for us to forgive those who do us wrong deeds. Being clean of demons on the inside, we have no resistance preventing forgiveness from manifesting in us as a lifestyle.

When we abide in the gospel, the Holy Spirit does not operate just on the outside of us as vessels; He steps right inside our hearts (the spiritual Holy of Holies) and dwell there to help us transact business with God.

He is here to change us from the inside out. He is not here to endorse the word of God under- written by the anointing designated to the first Adam. Rather, He is here solely to champion the cause of the word of God underwritten by the anointing designated to the second Adam—Jesus Christ. To this end, it becomes necessary for us to give Christianity its true definition below:

Christianity is having a belief in God, not by the commandments of God that came down to the Prophets in Israel, but the commandments of God that came down to the whole world by His only begotten Son, Jesus Christ, called the Gospel.

The former serves only to make us remain sin conscious. As a result, we keep a judgmental attitude towards other people and being always ready to find fault with them. The later serves to make us remain Son conscious. As a result, Jesus Christ is always on our minds. Daily, we learn to love and forgive people by the writ of the gospel of Jesus Christ, just as God in Christ loves and forgives us.

Welcome to the Christian Domain & Thinking

You shall Love the Lord your God with all your heart, with all your soul, with all your mind—this is the first and great commandment,

And the second is like it…

You shall Love your neighbor as yourself.

On these two commandments hang all the Law and the Prophets (Matthew 22:37-40)

We already have relationships with demons. Look at how things turned out for us in the world: corruption, murder, injustice and so forth.

Can we divorce the demons and fall in love all over again with God through Jesus Christ now?

Chapter One

The Doctrine of Jesus Christ (As the Beginning & the End) of the Gospel

All Scriptures of the Christian Bible Came From God But not all constitute the Gospel.

The Holy Bible is a book of many scriptures. In these scriptures, one finds both the Old Testament and the New Testament writings. The former, was largely written by Moses and the Prophets of old as inspired by God; whereas, the latter was written as an eyewitness account on the part of those that, with their own eyes, saw all that the Son of God performed in person, while He lived amongst the Jews on this earth for a little over 33 years.

With respect to the latter, it would interest one to note that the writings of the New Testament were, in a large part, verbatim out-takes, actual spoken words, delivered by the Son of God to the people. For the most part, Jesus Christ, the Son of God, clearly demonstrated the hidden fact that it was in His person that all the writings of the old were based. To that end, Jesus Christ would often choose the time of the Jewish feasts and the Sabbath days to perform miracles.

Although the religious sects amongst the Jews (Pharisees, Sadducees and Scribes) could not deny the evidence of the miracles, they were much perturbed since it occurred in violation of their religious laws as entrenched in the Old scriptures.

As a result, instead of rejoicing over these miracles and for the families that received them, the religious sects grew bitter, finding them to be repugnant. Instead of rejoicing over the person of Jesus Christ, a fellow Jew, endowed with such power to transform the lives of the people, they just straight-up hated

Him.

Instead of recognizing Him in their scriptures as the Messiah, they grew vastly at odds with Him. They even plotted how to seize Him and kill Him. At last, in the third year of His un-rivaled ministry, they succeeded. They hung Him on a wooden cross at Calvary.

Good riddance, they must have thought. Jesus Christ is dead and that's the end of it. At least now we can take back the people's hearts and restore our Old religious order.

But the contrary was true for them. Jesus Christ rose from the dead on the third day following His crucifixion. Jesus Christ spent another 40 days after resurrection in Jerusalem performing more signs and wonders before He was caught up at Mount Olivet into heaven in plain view of many eye-witnesses. Believe it or not, the story of Jesus Christ brings every listener or reader to this one conclusion: it was a life-giving, awesome and powerful ministry. Indeed, it was significantly different as it was powerful.

Chapter Two

The Superb Difference

It was superbly different in the sense that all His disciples, although brought up Jewish, once they switched their allegiance from the Old scriptures as a matter of faith and gave much heed to the Doctrine of Jesus Christ, also obtained the power (See the Acts of the Apostles). This power, however, was not something they flaunted on the outside of their garments or clothes. It all occurred on the inside of their living bodies. The only thing Jesus Christ required was that His disciples adhere strictly to His Doctrine.

They were to never deviate nor revert to the ways of the Old scriptures as a matter of faith. Such deviation, Jesus Christ maintained, would trigger a futile relationship with God.

He spoke to them the following words: "No one puts a piece from a new garment on an old one; otherwise the new makes a tear, and also the piece that was taken out of the new does not match the old. And no one puts new wine into old wineskins; or else the new wine will burst the wineskins and be spilled, and the wineskins will be ruined. But new wine must be put into new wineskins, and both are preserved. And no one having drunk old wine immediately desires new; for he says, "The old is better."
(Luke 5:36-39).

Stop for a minute and ponder on these words of Jesus Christ. What three things come out of it into your heart and mind? First, is it clear to you that the teachings of Jesus Christ is indeed the new wine? Second, do you get that, in its newness, it cannot be mixed with the old message or scriptures? Meaning, you cannot stand on them, preach them nor incorporate them into your prayers and your prayer life.

3

Such attempt by anyone will prove disastrous for both the preacher and the listener. In this case, the new wine is the Doctrine of Christ and the wineskin is the listener. Therefore, the new wine will burst the wineskin and be spilled, and the wineskin will be ruined. Hence, Jesus Christ emphasized that the new wine must be put into new wineskins and both are preserved. It is the only way the efficacy of the new wine (Doctrine) can be fully realized by both the preacher and the listener – not mixed together with the old.

The third thing in this discourse is aptly the fact of the hidden snare and the possible temptation: …no one having drunk old wine immediately desires new; for he says the old is better. I feel sad for him and for all others who hold the same view in the face of blatant spiritual wickedness in the world today. I therefore pray that they all repent and have life full of righteous power and possibilities, which are only found in Jesus Christ.

How did that grab you? Did I remotely sound like someone making a theological axiomatic statement? I mean—am I asking you to believe what I say without seeking proof for yourself?

No, I did not do that at all. Instead, I put it across to you as a theological dictum. I honestly and earnestly want you to see for yourself. I want you to deliberately switch your allegiance from the old scriptures to the new. I beseech you to sharpen your Christian instincts and virtues using the doctrine found in Matthew through the book of Revelation. Let the sub- sequent paragraphs engage your mind with the superb difference.

When you come to 2 Timothy 3:16 it reads, "…all scripture is given by inspiration of God, and is profitable for doctrine, for reproof, for correction, for instruction in righteousness, that the man of God may be complete, thoroughly equipped for every good work." If you were to stop here, you would then interpret its meaning out of context. As a result, you would think that this means go on mixing the old with the new. After all, it is written that all scripture is given by inspiration of God and is profitable....blah blah blah.

But you need to understand this: God is not the author of confusion. To this end, Paul the apostle, the same writer of the above message, now clarifies his position in 2 Corinthians 3:7-17. As you read on, you will come across these words, "unlike Moses who put a veil over his face so that the children of Israel could not look steadily at the end of what was passing away. But their minds were blinded. For until this day the same veil remains un-lifted in the reading of the Old Testament, because the veil is taken away in Christ. But even to this day, when Moses is read, a veil lies on their heart."

To me, the difference is now made abundantly clear. The Old scripture is not the Gospel. What is theologically alarming to me is the fact that it serves only to separate me from relating to God by virtue of the mentioned veil. Further, for me to even note that this veil lies across my heart just at the reading of the Old Testament is scary.

Therefore, since God cannot lie, I now bring this revealed knowledge to bear on my Christianity. I now bring my own faith under scrutiny. I start thinking like this: if as it is written that if you confess with your mouth the Lord Jesus and believe in your heart that God has raised Him from the dead, you will be saved, could there be a problem? Could there be a problem about my salvation since it hinges on one critical aspect: belief that must come from the heart?

What if, unbeknownst to me, due to my constant reading and practice of the Old, I have injured myself spiritually? Moreover, I am also taught by my Preacher that every prayer must end in Jesus' name, too. Or, I select my favorite scriptures from both the Old and New to chart my Christian course and walk. What do these things really mean to me and for my life in total?

Consequences

It does interest me to know that having a veil across my heart is not good news. I now sense that my ability to believe (also called faith) is gravely impacted. The veil shields me from receiving the things (teachings) of Christ. The things of Christ in turn serve to make me a Christian in truth. These things only take place deep inside my heart.

Chapter Three

The Real Meaning of Salvation

For one to really ascertain the real meaning of salvation, let's begin by sharing what salvation is not.

Salvation is not:

- Attending church on Sundays

- Maintaining a prayer meeting with a group of so- called believers

- Paying tithes/offerings to your church

- Moving in the gifts of the Holy Spirit in your church

- An ideology or a theological concept

- Something you put in work in order to earn; rather, the gospel asks you to work out your salvation with fear and trembling, implying that you already have it first.

What then is salvation? Look no further than in Romans 10:10 that says, "… for with the heart one believes unto righteousness and with the mouth confession is made unto salvation."

But in verse 9 it began with confess first, followed by believe in the heart. However, it ends verse 9 by saying you will be saved. Therefore, it is safe to posit that salvation is not secured from the emotional rush to confess the Lord Jesus without the sincere belief in the heart.

In God's book of life, it definitely takes both the heart and the mouth. Therefore, verse 10 now puts it in its correct order: **the**

heart that believes unto righteousness followed next by the mouth that now confesses all that the heart already believes.

Indeed, Jesus Christ puts it succinctly: For out of the abundance of the heart the mouth speaks. Read Matthew 12:34.

The Belief Factor in Salvation

When it comes to your salvation, belief is a process. It is not an instant grab-and-go ordeal. It is abundantly clear that many can think to come to God, but not many come to Jesus Christ. This fact is evident in the proliferation of religions in the world today. They all claim they serve God. But Christians know this truth: no one cometh unto the Father except by Jesus Christ. He is the way, the truth and the life. Jesus also says that no one can come to Him except the Father draws the person (John 6:44).

Without fail, when we come to Jesus Christ, we show up with two major issues: (1) a heart that is veiled, and (2) a spirit that is not His – an unclean spirit. That's how His work is cut out for Him. To get the job done which began since the fall of man, the heavenly Father equips the Son with a new word of life eternal and with His Spirit. That is why Jesus Christ truly stressed these main points in John 14 verses 10 and 24, respectively. In verse 10, He says, "I do not speak on my own authority; but the Father who dwells in me does the works." In verse 24, He also says, "he who does not love me does not keep my words; and the word which you hear is not mine but the Father's who sent me."

The word now takes on the all-encompassing role having the optimum sufficiency to tackle the two major issues of all human beings. On the part of the veil on the heart, one needs only to study the New Testament scriptures and retain them in the heart. On the part of getting rid of the unclean, evil spirit, one needs to again, study the New Testament scriptures and retain them in the heart. In doing so, you ultimately hear Jesus speak to your heart, for He says, "…the words I speak to you (John 6:63) they are spirit and they are life." Now enters faith and you become a new creation on the inside—a changed individual.

Chapter Four

The Supreme Benefit of Belief in the Gospel

The gospel, the New Testament or the Doctrine of Jesus Christ, carries with it one prime benefit, which is rated supreme in the eyes of God. For all intents and purposes, I want you to know that the supreme benefit of the gospel is that it generates perfected faith in the heart of the believer. This statement lends credence to the New Testament pronouncement that "…without faith it is impossible to please God."

(Hebrews 11: 6).

Do you wonder why I said perfected faith instead of just faith? This is because you might say that the scriptures of the Old Testament have presented Abraham and the likes as having faith in God, too. Besides, does not faith come (Romans 10: 17) by hearing and hearing by the word of God? As a result, you can opt to draw your faith also from reading the Old Testament. After all, it is also the word of God.

A big mistake you stand to make thinking in that manner. It simply shows you lack understanding, and you are likely to plunge headlong into spiritual jeopardy. But here is the truth: the word of God to those of Old had a limited scope in relation to the faith it generated in their hearts. As of the time of Moses and the Israelites, the word came to them by an angel named Jehovah. At the end of their time on the earth, all that their faith could yield them was a place in paradise, not heaven. They had no concept of the kingdom of God. Throughout their earthly lives, the word of God they received only served to ignite an inspired anticipation of the Messiah, who was to come, but had not yet arrived on the scene. They could only wait and wait.

On the contrary, you and I don't have to wait and wait for the

Messiah. The mystery of godliness (1 Timothy 3:16) is now in our time unraveled. God was manifested in the flesh, justified in the spirit, seen by angels, preached among Gentiles, believed on in the world and received up in glory. Hence, the word of God we have received comes not by inspiration, but first by manifestation.

To this end, the apostle John writes, "In the beginning was the word, and the word was with God and the word was God. He was in the beginning with God. All things were made through Him and without Him nothing was made that was made. In Him was life, and the life was the light of men... and the word became flesh and dwelt among us and we beheld His glory, the glory as of the only begotten of the Father, full of grace and truth. (John 1:1-3, 14)

The Son of God, who brought us the word for our time, in the Revelation 4, revealed God the Father to us whom we worship. He revealed both His ways and His heart to us, in John 3:16-17. In Matthew chapters 5, 6 and 7, He gave us the modalities of life necessary to qualify one to:

1.   Be perfect as the Father is perfect in all His ways

2.   Enter into the Kingdom of God and be in His presence, not in paradise

Owing to the fact that our faith is superior in quality, it became necessary for Jesus Christ to take this gospel and preach to the spirits in prison in Hades. According to 1 Peter 3:19-20 and 1 Peter 4:6 these were people of the Old Testament times. In order for them to be perfected like us and therefore enter into the kingdom, they had to accept Christ as their righteousness, too.

Seeing then all that God has done with this doctrine of Christ, it becomes clear that you and I will have no excuse if we fail to give our earnest heed to it. Hence, Jesus says, "...he who rejects me, and

11

does not receive my words has that which judges him: the word that I have spoken will judge him in the last day" (John 12:48).

Chapter Five

The Inalienable Authority of the Gospel

Beyond all controversy, the authority of the gospel is indeed inalienable. Inalienable means that it possesses such authority that nothing, no one or any other scripture/doctrine in the universe can take it away. Its inalienability has been fully established by three infallible proofs. For you to absolutely understand this point, I have to take you through some New Testament events for a minute.

Let's begin by bursting a huge theological myth going around in the churches today. Those who are totally drunk with the Old believe that Moses actually talked with God the Father during his Mount Sinai experience receiving the Ten Commandments. I would have you know that it is a big fat lie.

Search for yourself. In doing so, you will discover that in the original King James Version of the Bible, not the new King James, it is clearly stated (Exodus 3:2) that an angel of the Lord appeared to Moses in a flame of fire from a burning bush. Further, it is definitely made clear (Exodus 6:3) this same angel declares his name as Jehovah. Therefore, Jehovah is an angel, and not God the Father.

The gospel corroborates this alarming fact in two places:

First, in John 5:37 where Jesus says, "...and the Father Himself, who sent me, has testified of me. You have neither heard His voice at any time nor seen His form."

Second, in Hebrews 2:1-3, it says, "...for if the word spoken through angels proved steadfast and every transgression and disobedience received a just reward, how shall we escape if we neglect so great a salvation, which at first began to be spoken by the Lord..."

First Infallible Proof

The inalienable authority of the gospel is therefore established by our heavenly Father, the only Potentate, Righteous and True God, speaking, for the first time, out of heaven through the skies at the inception of the ministry of Jesus. As recorded in Matthew 3:17, 17:5 and in John 12:28 we read of the Father speaking audibly to the hearing of the people, endorsing His Son, whom He sent to save us. No created human being has ever heard His voice before according to Jesus (John 5:37). Prior to this event, Israelites were hearing the voices of angels.

As for His form, Jesus says, he who has seen me (John 14:9) has seen the Father. In addition, Revelations 4 paints a vivid picture of our heavenly Father for your perusal. Moses and the Jews saw such other forms including a pillar of clouds by day and a pillar of fire by night, fire in a burning bush orchestrated by angels (who disclosed their individual names to the Patriarchs) and not our heavenly Father.

Second Infallible Proof

The second viewpoint substantiating the inalienable authority of the gospel is apt to be the manifestation of the Son of God in the human flesh as Jesus Christ. As a result, the gospel, from its inception, installed a paradigm shift from being just another set of inspired holy writings to being God in a living person. Therefore, the gospel is personified in Jesus Christ. Simply put, you may recall John stating that "…the Word, who was God and was with God from the beginning, became flesh and dwelt among us and we beheld His glory as the only begotten of the Father"   (John 1:14).

In admonishing the Jews in relation to His authority, Jesus is heard saying, "…you search the scriptures for in them you think you have eternal life, and these are they which testify of me. But you are not willing to come to me that you may have life…Do not think that I shall accuse you to the Father, there is one who accuses you—Moses in whom you trust. For if you believed Moses, you would believe me, for he wrote about me. But if you do not believe his writings, how will you believe my words?" (John 5:39-47).

What exactly is Jesus Christ saying here to you and I? He wants the Jews and the rest of us professing Christians to now reckon that Moses, in all his writings of the Old as well as those scriptures, remain forever totally incapable of bequeathing to them or anyone else, anything they hoped for and/or could still be hoping for in God. Whether one seeks atonement or forgiveness of sins, righteousness or life beyond with God, it should be clear that only in Jesus and His doctrine/gospel can one get these things.

What accusation is Moses making against us to the Father? He is accusing us of being stubborn and stiff-necked. He is saying that we as sinners ought to be condemned for our sins. The language of his accusation is clear: he says we are rebels—just like at the waters of Meribah. He is saying we do not keep the law of atonement yearly as written. He is passing judgment of death on us for our sinful nature. He shows no mercy and no love towards us. But as a Christian, you have both heard and read that God is love.

Are you surprised about this revelation of Moses? You should not be. Right about now, you should be rejoicing having found out in time to come out of his doctrine before it is too late. Throughout his ministry, Moses had no means within himself to fix his raging temper tantrums. Regardless of how many times he and the Israelites offered up sacrifices to God for sins, their nature remained unchanged on the inside.

Neither he nor the people had it on the inside to love and hallow God from the heart. Better yet, he as their leader had not learned how to forgive his people. They made him angry with their constant murmurings over one thing or another.

Therefore, the Old Testament presents Moses (Numbers 20:1-13) committing the biggest mistake of his life: striking the rock twice with his rod when the Lord God asked him to speak to the rock, and it shall bring water for the people. Consequently, this act of Moses cost him dearly. God was in turn angry with him because he failed to believe God who said to speak to the rock.

Consequently, God barred Moses (Deuteronomy 34:1-8) from entering the promised land of Canaan. Moses lost out on that one thing he'd worked so hard for in the wilderness.

You and I should not end up like Moses. We will not if we yield to Christ. We are given everything Moses never had and did not know to ask for. In Christ, we receive the Holy Spirit—the helper on the inside of us all.

The Unequal Parallel

In the same breath, when you look at Jesus and Moses, you will find that the two share an unequal parallel. Moses ended his ministry in anger towards the people. God was not pleased with him. God barred him from entering Canaan. But Jesus ended his earthly ministry in forgiveness towards the people who actually plotted and nailed Him to the cross to die.

No wonder the Father spoke twice saying, "…this is my beloved Son in whom I am well pleased. Listen to Him"

(Matthew 3:17; 17:5).

Jesus opened His ministry teaching about love and forgiveness. Hence, the Father is well- pleased and makes it His good pleasure to give us the kingdom of His dear son.

No scripture in the Holy Bible presents this poignant, yet unequal parallel better than the case of the woman caught in the act of adultery by the Jews. Accordingly, the accusers said to Jesus, "'Moses in the law commanded us that such should be stoned. But what do you say?' First, Jesus stooped down and drew with His finger on the ground pretended He did not hear them. Then as they continued to ask, Jesus responded saying, 'He who is without sin among you, let him throw a stone at her first.'" The story ended thus: "Then those who heard it, being convicted by their conscience, went out one by one, beginning with the oldest even to the last. And Jesus was left alone, and the woman standing in the midst." (John 8:1-11).

Here, my dear friend is a clear and succinct demonstration of the inalienable authority of the gospel of Jesus Christ over all other scriptures in the Bible. The word of Jesus targets the conscience of a person to produce change. The change in question is for the betterment of the person. It starts from the inside of the individual. The accusers under doctrine of Moses or the Old Testament words/scriptures could not override the living words of Jesus, even in the glaring face of guilt gripping the guilty woman. On the contrary, the living words of Jesus swallowed up the Law of Moses and the Old scriptures to such a degree as to replacing them. Hence, the accusers bore witness of the truth in what Jesus said. Jesus talked to the unclean spirits inside of them and disarmed them, in essence. The words of Jesus are indeed spirit, and they are life.

Going back to Moses, Jesus presented him as an accuser to the Father of all those continuing and abiding in his doctrine purely in the interest of the gospel. Do not, I repeat, do not confuse

17

Moses with Satan, who is the accuser of the brethren. Jesus presented Moses in that light before His crucifixion at Calvary on the cross. The Jews under Moses did not know that they could not attain to righteousness via that old doctrine. Instead, their doctrine was about hard laws they could not keep and was not tending to grace. At this juncture, grace and truth just began with Jesus, and He was merely seeking to persuade them, with truth, to embrace the new and living way. Therefore, Jesus also said in another place that **He "... did not come to destroy the law and the prophets but to fulfill them"   (Matthew 5:17).**

Moses the law-giver and Elijah the prophet spent their entire lifetimes on earth never hearing the gospel message of Jesus Christ. Since the gospel came way after their time, both of them departed this life still indulging in their respective ministry. As a result, their spirits were not perfected yet. For this cause, God the Father had to present the Son, whose spirit is perfect, to both Moses and Elijah (Matthew 17: 1-5) at the Mount of Transfiguration.

Additionally, before Jesus rose on the third day following His crucifixion, He spent the two days of his burial in the grave. During this time, He was busy preaching this same gospel (1Peter 3:19-20, 4:6) to those in Hades and to those in paradise, under Abraham's bosom. In doing so, Jesus extended the grace to them so that they could receive the righteousness of God and be perfected in spirit.

When the church is caught up into the clouds to be with the Lord, Moses and Elijah, the two witnesses, shall no doubt return to the earth, according to Revelations 11. At that time, their testimony will be purely about this gospel and no other doctrine. This truly leaves you with spiritual food for thoughts as to how you should regard and handle this doctrine of Christ. Like it or not, it remains an inextricable part of everyone's life, period. It is true for those who are alive and equally true for those who are dead. It is so indispensable to your life and mine that Paul made this pronouncement to the Galatians church: "But even if we or an angel from heaven preach any other gospel to you than what we have preached to you, let him be accursed" (Galatians 1:6-9).

I believe Jesus when He says that Moses is accusing the Jews and the followers of that old doctrine before the Father. My confidence in such a belief stems from the following: the last thing of sacramental proportion that Jesus did before He died, which He says He will do first in the kingdom when we (the church) meet up over there with Him.

That last thing, which shall be first, that you ought to know, is the taking of Communion. Are you surprised? If so, then read Matthew 26: 26-29. In verse 29 Jesus says, "But I say to you, I will not drink of this fruit of the vine from now on until that day when I drink it new with you in my Father's kingdom."

This is invariably the unequal parallel to Moses seeing that his last work in his ministry was to accuse the Israelites during the waters of Meribah. That's all he continued doing since he never yet received the gospel of Christ until after Jesus preached to him before the resurrection of the Lord on the third day.

The Third Infallible Proof

The third infallible proof of the inalienable authority of the gospel, above all other scriptures in the Bible, is the promise and the manifestation of the third person of the Godhead: The Holy Spirit. As a biblical phenomenon, this event unfolded in this present world (just two thousand years ago in Jerusalem) in two phases such as (1) the Promise phase, and (2) the Manifestation phase, respectively.

The Promise Phase

If you were to ask me, it is most probable that I would tell you the news of the Holy Spirit came as a total surprise to His disciples. Why were they surprised, you ask? You check it out. Jesus and the twelve disciples had been together for at least three years. During this time of His ministry, Jesus made no mention of the Holy Spirit. Then suddenly, after they had the famous last supper, taken what is known in the church now as the Communion, Jesus broke the news of the Holy Spirit to them walking toward the garden of Gethsemane.

In doing so, He said the following, "If you love me, keep my commandments. And I will pray the Father and He will give you another Helper that He may abide with you forever—the Spirit of truth, whom the world cannot receive, because it neither sees Him nor knows Him; but you know Him, for He dwells with you and will be in you." (John 14:15-17).

Hearing this for the first time must have been mind boggling for the disciples of Jesus. Jesus is telling them He must go away to the Father and leave them with the task of unraveling the mystery of the Holy Spirit. It is safe to deduce that the disciples began wrestling in their minds how they were to relate to the Holy Spirit. However, they were really not ready for the magnitude of events that ensued consequent to all that Jesus kept teaching them. On the one hand, Jesus let them know (John 16:7-15) that when the Holy Spirit comes, He will convict the world of (1) sin, (2) righteousness, and (3) judgment. In explaining Himself further to the disciples, Jesus stated the following:

- Of sin, because they do not believe in me

- Of righteousness, because I go to the Father and you see me no more

- Of judgment, because the ruler of this world is already judged.

On the other hand, as far as His disciples were concerned; Jesus said when the Holy Spirit has come, He will do the following:

- He will guide them into all truth for He will not speak on His own authority; but whatever He hears He will speak and will tell them things to come.

- He will glorify Jesus, for He will take of what is Christ's and declare it to them.

Permit me to indulge your Christ-loving mind just a little here. Would you say that you've noticed two phrases highlighted in this section? These two highlighted phrases represent the modus operandi of the Holy Spirit, according to Jesus Christ. I mean that when He comes, He will (1) be in us, and (2) take of what is Jesus Christ's and declare it to us. For you, me and everyone else in Christianity, this information is pertinent indeed.

This information on the Holy Spirit not only impacts our Christianity, it totally goes beyond to establish our salvation, as well as maintain it in perpetuity. On this particular promise is the hope and God's will of forming and establishing a church anchored. The work of the Holy of the Spirit equips the body of Christ for every good work. On this particular promise is anchored the resurrection power for those who died or will die in Christ, as well as the changing—within a twinkle of an eye, those alive and remaining for the rapture.

Clearly, you now know that He is to come and will be in you. Clearly, you now know while He is in you, He will only take of what is Christ's and declare it to you. Clearly, you now know what is of Christ is nothing other than the gospel/doctrine.

And Jesus forbade every believer to mix it with the scriptures of the Old Testament. With that in mind, I'd like to present to you a theological hypothesis.

Take for instance a Christian whose knowledge of the things of God emanates from the scriptures of the Old Testament. This person understands all the types and the shadows of Christ from Genesis to Malachi. This person has the uncanny ability to memorize and regurgitate the words of the old prophets the likes of Isaiah, Joshua, Ezekiel, Hosea, Malachi and so forth. Do you think that this is the model Christian whom the Holy Spirit will come and take these things of God on the inside of this person and declare to him or her? I certainly think not.

My confidence in the above assessment is strictly biblical, not opinion-based. Yes these scriptures of old came from God. But as Jesus Christ has come already in the flesh, these scriptures exist as mere letters having not the spirit of God in them. Meaning, these old scriptures do not engender, in any way shape or form, real intimacy between a person and God. This is what God looks for to accomplish in this particular dispensation known as the church age.

That is why Jesus strictly forbade anyone mixing his words/scriptures with the old. His words, Jesus says are given to Him by the Father. His words, Jesus says are spirit and life. This means they are not mere letters. The spirit of the heavenly Father resonates in them, meaning the doctrine of Christ serves to engender real intimacy with God. The church, in turn, becomes the bride of Christ as a result.

In the natural, the word bride carries a certain, peculiar connotation. For all intents and purposes, you will agree that it triggers in the mind the notion of a relationship. Not just a platonic relationship, but an intimate one. In this case, it involves the couple spending real

22

quality time alone together. Perhaps, they can find the moment to be ripe for fondling as in hugging and kissing. Perhaps, they can find the moment to be ripe for a cool pillow-talk conversation. There are no holds barred in this precious moment of intimate conversation by the couple. They can selectively talk about anything or totally everything on their minds. One cannot go wrong having no ill will towards the other partner. One has total liberty with the other.

You are not afraid to get undressed in the presence of your significant other. You remain receptive to each other. You both share some deep-seated secrets, even those from childhood. You both want the best for each other. All these fonder experiences now culminate to an epitome in us, in the natural, called marriage. Now when the bride continues to wear a veil over her face, long after the wedding has been concluded, don't you think that there is a problem with that bride? Most certainly, I say. For one thing, the veil conceals her facial beauty and adorable facial features from her groom so that he cannot clearly behold. The other thing is that the veil totally gets in the way of sweet kisses that could be placed on her lips from time to time as is always the case in romance.

As time passes, in this weird state of existence, the couple is gripped with emotional strains often associated with lack of satisfaction. In the end, they grow apart as if they never knew each other. Hence, Jesus gave us Matthew 7: 21-27 for our individual introspection.

Spiritually speaking, it would interest you to know that Christianity is totally couched on the same premise as in creating symmetry in relationship with Christ. In this holy, revered regard, everything culminates to an epitome in heaven, in the spiritual, called worship. To this end, Jesus therefore says, "But the hour is coming and now is when the true worshipers will worship the Father in sprit and truth; for the

Father is seeking such to worship Him. God is a spirit and they that worship Him must worship Him in spirit and in truth.' Oh yes, the Father is definitely seeking such Christians to worship Him"   (John 4:23-24).

You would recall that Jesus spoke these words to the woman at the well, the essence being that God deliberately went to her in order to point us all to its spiritual implications. Indeed, our Christian life reveals an irrefutable correlation to hers on so many levels. Hers occurs in the natural; whereas, ours take place spiritually. Naturally, she had been in intimate relationships five times with five different husbands. Spiritually, we too have been in and out of real intimate relationship with Christ many times and still counting.

Some days, we read the Old Testament to falsely and erroneously build our faith in God. Other days, we read the New Testament where our Christian faith is truthfully formed and perfected in God.

Then we spiritually mix the blood of animals with the perfect blood of Christ, ignorantly, as we worship God. Seeing now that God totally and unequivocally objects, what does it say about our romance status with Him? Is it not just as bouncy as the woman at the well?

Truly, our romance is not on a sure and steady course. It remains bumpy and fragmented. We are in and out with little or nothing to show for it, in the kingdom of God. When we assemble together as a church, we congregate under a spiritually segregated atmosphere of worship.

For this reason, Jesus minced no words when He told the people, "These people draw near to me with their mouths. And honor me with their lips. But their hearts are far from me. And in vain they worship me, teaching as doctrines the commandments of men"
                                                    (Matthew 15: 8-9).

Here, our Lord Jesus to all worshipers, carefully reveals the gravity, as well as the travesty of our Christianity. Therefore, since I now clearly see the link between the two, it is safe for me to deduce that **Christianity not based on and not emanating from the doctrine of Jesus Christ, is no Christianity at all.**

Why would I be so bold to say that? You can clearly see that the key items necessary for salvation such as (1) the heart, and (2) the mouth are brought under scrutiny. Your Holy Bible tells you that with the heart one believes unto righteousness and with the mouth one confesses unto salvation.

If your heart is far from Him because you do not have His word in you, how can you truly be saved? As for me and my household, we do not want to spend all our earthly years worshipping God in vain. We want the doctrine of Christ. We vehemently reject the doctrine of men.

The Manifestation Phase

The person of the Holy Spirit, though invisible, made a grand entrance in Jerusalem to 120 disciples, a mixed crowd, two thousand years ago. According to the gospel, the day of this glorious manifestation of the Holy Spirit is called Pentecost. But why should you be remotely convinced? To what can this invisible phenomenon be compared?

For starters, let's recall the recent earthquake that rocked the country of Haiti in January 2010. The force and the power of its thrust coupled with the carnage it brought to the citizenry will live in infamy for generations. Haitians will never forget it. That is the power of an invisible force of nature in action that will help you to begin to fathom, in contrast, the reality of Pentecost.

Due to the fact that the earth is at this time swallowed up and enveloped in evil and wickedness, every invisible force originating from it will almost always bring about death. This fact holds true, you would agree, for invisible wind forces such as hurricanes, tornados and so forth. The folks in Key West, Florida, can attest to such recurring reality since they face it year after year. Please do not tell me that you have forgotten already all that hurricane Katrina did to the good folks in New Orleans, Louisiana. To this day, the state government of Louisiana is still counting the cost resulting from the damage.

On the contrary, the Pentecost experience was similar in terms of wind force, but with a positive outcome. No one died as is often the case with natural forces. Instead, those to whom He came became animated and were transformed. Those who then witnessed the transformation of the 120 believers and disciples marveled and were intrigued by the experience.

Pentecost as I would have you know was a supernatural occurrence. Its place of origin is heaven, not earth as coming from the skies above. It is the one and only human experience that attests the release of God the Spirit from the Father to us on the earth, which Jesus promised. Below is how the Bible gives the account to the whole world:

> When the day of Pentecost had fully come, they were all with one accord in one place. And suddenly there came a sound from heaven, as of a rushing mighty wind, and it filled the whole house where they were sitting. Then there appeared to them divided tongues, as of fire, and one sat upon each of them. And they were all filled with the Holy Spirit and began to speak with other tongues, as the Spirit gave them utterance.
>
> And there were dwelling in Jerusalem Jews, devout men, from every nation under heaven. And when this sound occurred, the multitudes came together and were confused because everyone heard them speak in his own language. Then they were all amazed and marveled, saying to one another, "Look are not all these

who speak Galileans? And how is it that we hear each in our own language in which we were born? Parthian and Medes and Elamites, those dwelling in Mesopotamia, Judea and Cappadocia, Pontus and Asia, Phrygia and Pamphylia, Egypt and the parts of Libya adjoining Cyrene, visitors from Rome, both Jews and proselytes, Cretans and Arabs—we hear them speaking in our own tongues the wonderful works of God."

So they were all amazed and perplexed saying to one another, "Whatever could this mean?" Others who were mocking said, "They are full of new wine."

(Acts 2:1-13).

Interestingly enough, the various groups of eyewitnesses in Jerusalem commented that the disciples and believers were full of new wine.

Would you not agree that the word New Wine is intrinsic to the Pentecost experience? Further, the Galileans spoke with new tongues, the birth languages of these witnesses, which they never studied nor learned.

As you can imagine, the Pentecost experience totally flies in the face of fiction or myth. Unlike an inexplicable act of nature riddled with damages of sort, Pentecost was the opposite.

The eyewitnesses, upon the aftermath of Pentecost, did not run around rescuing survivors and the wounded. They did not spread open gurneys to transport injured folks to a makeshift triage unit. Yes, cloven tongues of fire, reminiscent of the time of Moses, rested upon the heads of the believers and disciples, but they were not burnt. I remember Moses having his own experience with fire signifying the presence of God. The fire in question alighted upon a bush and burned without consuming

27

the bush. The fire did not rest on Moses at all, but on the bush. The phenomenon intrigued Moses and caused him to draw near and hear the voice of the angel – Jehovah.

Unlike the time of Moses when God dealt with people from a distance, Pentecost demonstrated something new. The fire as the Spirit of God rested on the people thus making them figuratively the 'burning bush' arousing he curiosity of the eyewitnesses in Jerusalem. Moreover, instead of hearing the voice of an angel, they heard voices of their native tongues spoken by the believers and disciples, the wonderful works of God.

In Pentecost God was not operating any longer from the outside of human beings, but from the inside of people. Pentecost serves best to suggest that God now wants a close- knit relationship with mankind as in intimacy. In doing so, God used the varied indigenous languages of the eye-witnesses as a clear sign, which speaks for unity of all tongues, tribes and nations. As people, we can only relive this experience and achieve this goal by virtue of the gospel of Jesus Christ.

Chapter Six

The Implications of the Gospel on Christianity

I would be totally remiss if I did not insert this thought on your mind: **All scriptures of the Christian Bible came from God, but not all constitute the gospel.** It is something more of a lifestyle than a religion. It receives the full endorsement of the Godhead—the Father, the Son, and the Holy Spirit, given the inalienable authority of the gospel over and above the other bible scriptures. Further, a central facet of Christianity is that it speaks for change.

In terms of this change, it implies one having to undergo a renaissance of sort, learning the scriptures all over again with utmost diligence. In doing so, one now discovers or rediscovers the change in question, which serves to redefine the gospel. I am indeed a graduate of the renaissance experience spoken of here and I move to redefine the gospel from my ordained, yet humble perspective. The definition is as follows: **The gospel is the manner, the form, and the style, which God has undertaken to fulfill all the promises (to the fathers and prophets of old) of salvation and eternal life for the Jews and Gentiles in the world.** I speak to you about something entrenched in the core nature of God called love. It is love that sponsored the change.

Therefore, instead of an eye for an eye way of life of the old, the gospel (John 3:16-17) says, "For God so loved the world that He gave His only begotten Son that whosoever believes in Him should not perish but have everlasting life. For God did not send His Son into the world to condemn the world, but that the world through Him might be saved." This indeed speaks of the invariable, personal involvement of the Holy Father with humanity in contrast to the old. This is good news indeed. In essence, by virtue of embracing the gospel, sin is not imputed to anyone who does.

To demonstrate His love commitment to the world, the Holy Father put His Holy moves on the Virgin Mary. In doing so, He intercepted an earthly love affair between the Virgin Mary and Joseph and intimately elevated it. In doing so, God spiritually joined heaven and earth. He then consummated the union by planting His Holy seed in the womb of the Virgin Mary. In doing so, the birth of the gospel was underway.

I speak to you about the Holy Seed of God in human form: Jesus Christ. In confirming this truth, the scriptures point to the actions of Simeon, who handled the dedication of the eight-day-old baby boy Jesus in the temple at Jerusalem. Simeon was just and devout. He was waiting for the con- solation of Israel, and the Holy Spirit was upon him. It had been revealed to him by the Holy Spirit that he would not see death before he had seen the Lord's Christ.

On the day of the dedication, he came by the Spirit into the temple. When Mary and Joseph brought in the child Jesus to do for Him according to the custom of the law, Simeon took Him up in his arms and blessed God saying: "Lord, now you are letting your servant depart in peace, according to your word. For my eyes have seen your salvation which you have prepared before the face of all peoples. A light to bring revelation to the Gentiles and the glory of your people Israel." (Luke 2:21-32).

Clearly, Simeon's prayer is telling of the fulfillment of God's promise to the prophets and fathers of old of the salvation of the people in the person of the child Jesus. Being convinced by the Spirit that Jesus was the one, Simeon then rejoiced. In other words, Simeon was simply spending his life in the temple waiting.

I speak to you in regards to Jesus' particular or characteristic way of acting and speaking to the people in Jerusalem and the surrounding regions.

His acts were phenomenal, and His speeches unraveled the eternal mystery of the word known as God. Taken together, everything about Jesus Christ pointed to and was synonymous with change—change in the people's view of God and change in how people ought to see one another.

Invariably, Jesus' teaching was about change in one's view of God. I mean that we ought to know that God comprises three persons: Father, Son and Holy Spirit.

Jesus' teachings were also about change in one's view of people in general—that we ought not see the people around us as enemies, but as neighbors to love and care about. His teaching was also about change in one's view of worship and prayer. As for worship, Jesus says it is no longer done at Mt. Sinai or in Jerusalem, but in our own individual closets at our own homes.

Jesus taught us God's approved prayer format. In this format, He helps us restore what Moses failed to do during the waters of Meribah in the desert: to hallow God. This is something our heavenly Father holds in high regard.

Our heavenly Father places such a high premium on this that when Moses failed to hallow Him, it cost Moses:

(1) His ministry reward of the promise land

(2) His life—for Moses died at Mt. Nebo blocked by God from crossing into Canaan.

This incident as well as its corresponding misfortune has remained forever in my book the biggest spiritual mistake of Moses.

But we give heartfelt and sincere thanks to Jesus, who has come and taught us how to pray and how to hallow God's name.

In His teachings, Jesus put forth the following: "Our Father who art in heaven. Hallowed be thy name. Thy kingdom come. Thy will be done on earth as it is in heaven. Give us this day our daily bread and forgive us our trespasses as we forgive those who trespass against us. Lead us not into temptation but deliver us from evil. For thine is the kingdom, power and the glory forever. Amen." (Matthew 6: 9-13).

Jesus' teaching was about change in one's view of the Sabbath. Jesus Christ wanted us to know that the Sabbath was created for man, not man for Sabbath. Simply put, it is the one day out of the seven days where God and man connect and commune, before man gets back on the rhythm and the rigor of earthly life and living again. Six days were for the bulk of working. One day was set aside for the Lord. In other words, Sabbath was created for man to be refreshed, healed and restored by God. It was not meant for man to cease from work, sit and remain idle the entire day. Even the Jews knew it was impossible to do absolutely nothing on the Sabbath since they fetched water for their donkeys, too.

Therefore, when Jesus came on the scene, His style, which the Jews saw as breaking their law of Sabbath, gave rise to the following Sabbath-day controversies:

- Sabbath day healing of the man with the withered hand (Mark 3: 1- 6, Matthew 12: 9-14)

- Sabbath day healing of the man by Bethesda at Jerusalem (John 5:1- 13)

- Sabbath day plucking and eating of grains from the field by His disciples (Luke 6:1-5)

- Sabbath day healing of the woman stricken with a spirit of infirmity who remained bent over for 18 years unable to raise herself up (Luke 13: 10-17)

Indeed, all these examples revealed how God intended man to keep the Sabbath. No one else is holy except God. Therefore, keeping your Sabbath day holy is to spend time and commune with Christ. You will find that Christ will meet up with you. God uses Sabbath to refresh, heal and restore people. That is why He created it for man. That is why He created it for you.

Jesus' teaching was about change in one's view of temple. I mean that neither the Jews nor anyone in the world are to be oblivious to the true temple in which God absolutely dwells here on earth. Until Jesus came into the world, the Jews never conceptualized a human being as a temple of God. To them as well as all others still operating on the periphery of the gospel, a temple was literally the man- made building constructed with wooden beams, cement/stucco walls, zinc-and-tile roof. In other words, it was a construct borne out of the human intellect. It was adorned with geometric rows of nice sitting pews followed by ceiling fans, air-conditioning units, lightings, leadership sitting area and the preaching podium.

When the people congregate, whether a small or a large group, for worship service, the irony was that God's presence was strictly by virtue of the people moving in the gifts of the Holy Spirit, independent of all the man-made stuff in the temple.

In all my church life, I have yet to see a pew or a ceiling fan get up and prophesy and /or give a word of knowledge to a member. Just because the location of the church building is fixed and designated for the congregation to meet regularly, it wrongly leaves people with the illusion that such is the only place to meet with God.

Regrettably, they rob God of the eternal chance of dwelling and being present in them, the people. Instead, they try to confine the almighty God to dwell in their lifeless, inanimate church buildings. Seeing therefore that this ignorance has gone on too long, the Father sent Jesus to come and correct it. To accomplish it, Jesus did the following:

> Now the Passover of the Jews was at hand and Jesus went up to Jerusalem. And He found in the temple those who sold oxen and sheep and doves and the money-changers doing business. When He had made a whip of cords, He drove them all out of the temple with the sheep and the oxen, and poured out the changers' money and overturned the tables. And He said to those who sold doves, 'Take these things away. Do not make my Father's house a house of merchandise.' Then the disciples remembered that it was written, 'Zeal for your house has eaten me up.' So the Jews answered and said to Him, 'What sign do you show to us since you do these things?' Jesus answered and said to them, '**Destroy this temple and in three days I will raise it up**.' Then the Jews said, 'It has taken forty-six years to build this temple and will you raise it up in three days?' But He was speaking of the temple of His body'
>
> (John 2:13-22).

As you can see, Jesus clearly instituted a complete paradigm shift. Accordingly, the reasoning of the Jews was earth-based; whereas the reasoning of Jesus is the view of the Father and all of heaven. All the scriptures show that God does not dwell in temples made by men's hands. Therefore, for anyone to posit that the temple of greater value to God is the inanimate buildings made by man is indeed a farce.

In the days of Moses, God not having His true human temple to dwell in yet, set up His presence in the tabernacle as a pillar of cloud or fire to the Israelites. In the days of the prophets, God, who did not yet dwell in them caused His spirit to come upon them on the outside. After the mission was accomplished, the Spirit then departed from the prophet.

Conversely, God used the birth, life and times of Jesus in the human flesh on the earth to up the ante, allowing His Holy Spirit to dwell on the inside of a living person forever. The way God the Father operated in the life of Christ throughout His stay on the earth, is the way He lives in and with the rest of us, as we believe in Jesus.

To accomplish this task, God sets up a living, workable spiritual tool. That tool that invites the Holy Spirit to come inside of you is indeed the gospel/doctrine of Jesus Christ. Through the gospel/doctrine of Jesus, we the believers graduate from our natural state to the kingdom state of existence.

Our Natural State of Existence

No empirical data whether from the sciences or any other school of human thought has revealed the hidden mystery of the spiritual nature of human life. No medical doctor has been able to unravel the mystery behind the vital organs in the human body. These indispensable and equally brilliant people in the medical field, in all their good works, can only discover the ongoing phenomena within the human body and report on it.

For example, in their scientific research, they discover that:

1. The human heart is alive and it pumps blood that supplies the whole body

2. The human brain is alive and it is the information center which sends and receives messages for the optimum functioning of the entire body

3. Our sensory organs serve us well

But beyond all that, my question for you still remains: What makes the heart, the brain, and the sensory organs have life in the first place? Why does God bother much with humanity given that He has innumerable legions of angels in heaven that serve and worship Him?

The answer to the first question is the spirit within a person gives life to the organs and keeps the person alive. My answer to the first question as herein stated is biblically corroborated in James 2:26. In this particular gospel according to James, it is written as follows: "**For as the body without the spirit is dead**...." This divine revelation lends much credence to the findings from my research on the behavioral dynamics of human beings and living creatures. **In conclusion, the research gave birth to what I called the Psychodynamics Theory of human behavior.** The theory says: *For every human action, there is an equal and originating thought. As a trigger, the thought is strictly a function of the Spirit within the person.* - Lloyd Nsek Sr

The answer to the second question is similar to the first, but much focused in this regard: God is absolutely interested in what manner of spirit is in a person.

Many people all over the world live oblivious to this reality and mystery surrounding our God-given human nature. They are totally clueless of the nature of human beings. Simply put, it would interest us to understand the human construct. The human being is fearfully and wonderfully made by Christ the Creator.

A human being is created to remain a storehouse for more than just organs and body parts. It is created to carry spirits on the inside, whose function is to enliven and enable the different organs and parts to work.

However, there is something critical for you to note: these organs work in accordance with the agenda of the resident spirit(s) in that person.

In other words, if the resident spirit in a person is evil, the brain is therefore going to produce evil/wicked thoughts with corresponding cruel, stupid and unconscionable behaviors.

Conversely, if the resident spirit is holy or good, the result is likewise praise-worthy, and there is peace on the inside.

The gospel, my friend, is the only scripture that brought this great insight about human nature to the world. For this cause, Jesus says:

> "When an unclean spirit goes out of a man, he goes through dry places seeking rest and finds none. Then he says, 'I will return to my house from which I came.' And when he comes, he finds it empty, swept and put in order. Then he goes and takes with him seven other spirits more wicked than himself and they enter and dwell there; and the last state of that man is worse than the first. So shall it also be with this wicked generation"   (Mathew 12:43).

Notice phrases such as ….unclean spirit goes out of a man …return to my house from which I came …enter and dwell there …last state of that man is worse than the first. Taken together, it speaks volumes about the natural state of existence of a human being. Jesus used this revelation to emphasize our need for the right or the clean spirit: The Holy Spirit.

Consider that while the unclean spirit remains in a person, whether one or up to seven, nothing good comes through this person. But while he or she lives his or her natural life in the human flesh, the following behaviors and habits are clearly seen: "adultery, fornication, uncleanness, lewdness, idolatry, sorcery, hatred, contentions, jealousies, outbursts of wrath, selfish ambitions, dissensions, heresies, envy, murders, drunkenness, revelries, and the like" (Galatians 5:19-21).

Are any of these present in your life? If you find out that even though you do not or in some cases cannot physically experience any of these, but in your mind you hold the thoughts or daydream them, then your brain is under the influence of an unclean spirit. If for instance, you do not murder anyone, but you simply hate a person or a race of people, then you should beware and bring yourself to a solemn psychoanalysis session. This way, you can deduce that your brain and your heart have been hijacked and are functioning in pursuit of the agenda of the spirit within you.

This phenomenon in human nature is what underscores the schisms and mayhems in the world. As a result, countless wars are fought, won and lost, all for selfish ambitions of couples, neighbors, and nations.

In the world of biological sciences with emphasis on human existence and development, we find characters the likes of Charles Darwin, who put forth the erroneous Evolution theory. That theory, in my view, is erroneous in the sense that it fails to address a key ingredient necessary to support it. It fails to demonstrate how the theory continues to operate. (To be true, the theory must be continuing in effect.) But there is a fatal disconnect in the evolution chain as it has been spelled out thus far.

For example, every animal species in the evolution chain stopped on a dime from morphing into a different kind of animal and began procreating after its own specific kind. In other words, the tadpole of a frog or a toad ceased from changing into a monkey and then into becoming a man/woman. Instead, these species have continued on living and reproducing after their own kind. Again, it was the spirit in Charles Darwin that caused his God-given brain to hold and produce such a morbid theory.

Another classic case in point is the legacy of Mr. Adolf Hitler of Germany. Who amongst us as far back as the 1940-1945, can ever forget the atrocities of the Second World War? Hollywood has done a fantastic job of portraying the different faces and facets of the WWII years. Besides his hatred for the Jewish people and his delusion of world conquest, he also came up with a sinister scheme to inaugurate a different, perfect race of people in Germany. In this odious scheme, he went on to select choice-and-able males and females to couple them. In this union, these couples were to reproduce blond hair and blue-eyed children. They were to be known as the Arian race.

Now my friend, there is nothing wrong with one having an imagination. There is also nothing wrong with one running with the imagination. But when the imagination serves to reveal, at best, your own hatred for yourself, then it is a problem. As I tell you this, recall that Mr. Adolf Hitler was born having brunette hair with brown eyes. Hence, contrary to who he was physically as a person, he was prepared to alter the human race entirely if only he could.

What a travesty for Mr. Hitler. In the context of Matthew 12: 43-45 Jesus shows that the spirit in us in our natural state of existence tends toward evil. Even if we are sometimes nice to one another, such niceness is insufficient to make us good, given the ultimate selfish, wicked agenda of the resident spirit lurking on the inside. To this end, Jesus (Matthew 7:11) says, "If you then being evil know how to give good gifts to your children, how much more will your Father who is in heaven give good things to those who ask Him." By a shared implication, both Charles Darwin and Mr. Adolf Hitler represent, as living proofs, the effects generated by unclean spirits in a person.

As you can imagine, even though each had both the brain and the heart, the spirit within them used these organs to purport big fat lies. Darwin came to the realization that he had a father and a mother who gave natural birth to him. Further, having his children therefore meant he would find a beautiful young lady to couple with, have sexual intercourse and get her pregnant. In doing so, he had the pleasure of finding out the sole function of the male penis and the female vagina in the context of natural life, according to creation not evolution. Accordingly, he had to wait nine months for the vaginal delivery of his child by his woman, just like he was born to his parents. He did not have to pick up a tadpole from the lake and nurse it to the point where it changed into a monkey awaiting his return from work one day to call him daddy.

Darwin never dragged anyone or any nation to war like Hitler. It is most probable that Darwin was kind to his folks and to those whom he worked with. But telling them such a big fat lie as the Evolution Theory is indeed evil. It shows without a doubt that the spirit that was in him was a lying spirit. That spirit was all about lies, and not the spirit of truth.

Another situation that we are grappling with these days is the issue of gay and lesbian marriages. That concept of life and lifestyle is definitely triggered by the spirit within them. On a closer look into it, this lifestyle completely alters their natural tendencies and affections. As a result, a gay or a lesbian person does not channel his or her natural sensual, passionate affections toward the opposite sex. Instead, a gay or lesbian person gravitates toward another of the same sex and gender. Simply put, a gay guy is affectionately drawn to another male person; whereas a lesbian is likewise affectionately drawn to another female person.

The irony entrenched in this lifestyle is that even though these couples practice homosexuality some still desire have and nurture children—a normal product of a heterosexual union. They want to lead a normal life while living as they have chosen. They want as well as demand a family. Even though their peculiar lifestyle is the antithesis of the natural order, these people want to bring up children, who may walk about with lots of incorrectly answered questions in this world.

Consider a major city in the United States like New York or Los Angeles. Picture two children in kindergarten. The first child comes from a family, whose father and mother are male and female and love the child much. The second child's parents are two women, who love their child very much, too. During recess, the first child, who has bonded in friendship with the second child, speaks in glowing terms about how her daddy spends so much time in front of the mirror trimming his mustache to keep it even as the first day from the barber shop.

Of course, this is strange to the second child. There is no man figure with her parents. As for the word mustache, she never heard of it. Consequently, when one of her female parents comes to pick her up from school, she can't wait to share the story from her newfound friend with the parent. Upon arriving home, she followed her female parent to the mirror in the room.

Looking at her parent's face in the mirror, she now asks, "Mommy, what is a mustache?"

Before the parent can answer, she asks another question, "How come my other mommy don't have one?"

An awkward moment like this is commonplace in relation to this lifestyle, in my view. Take for instance, their plan of having a baby and bringing that to fruition. To succeed, they must resort to sperm donor arrangements from male donors. In the case of lesbians, the fact that they are females really proves that they are indeed living a lie. In their own lesbian case, neither of the two females can augment sperm needed to fertilize the egg in the womb. Likewise, in the case of a gay couple, neither of the two males can augment the egg nor carry a womb to sustain pregnancy. Therefore, seeing their obfuscated way of life being totally skewed from the natural order, it is safe for you to conclude that it is a function of the twisted spirit inside of them.

The Kingdom State of Existence

By its name, I will not blame you if, in your mind, it denotes a nation or a country with an authority figure the like a king or a ruler with many subjects. As is always the case in a typical kingdom, those governed report to the king. They show their piety and pay their homage or obeisance to the king according to the governing laws of the kingdom. As you can imagine, the foregoing constitutes, the makings of an ideal kingdom, and you and I cannot vouch for its existence here on this present earth.

Some vouchsafed examples in this present earth are the ones peopled by war-mongering kings or corrupt totalitarian presidents. Whatever form of government the kingdom espouses, be it democracy or theocracy, the quality of life of the people within remains stifled resulting from the selfishness that exists. Consequently, people are not living fulfilled lives.

The kingdom state of existence I am talking about here is not procured by the proliferation of organized religions in the country. Heaven knows, and you also know that not all those who say, "Lord" really do the Lord's will. In the case of the churches, you will find that each denomination is operating on a slightly different standard from the others.

The Catholics cannot function save for the molten crucifix of Jesus Christ. Despite the fact and the biblical truth of His resurrection, they still leave Jesus hanging on their Catholic cross. It is largely their physical, visible worship object amid the array of other sculptured stone images of angels and celestial personalities scattered across many of their church grounds. It is sold in tiny figurine forms as paraphernalia used by the converts throughout the global Catholic kingdom. Further, the Catholics deify the Virgin Mary, the earthly mother of Jesus Christ. Now, on this particular matter of the deity of the Virgin Mary, I have the honor of telling you that it is indeed a stretch. As you can already deduce, there is a spirit running the Catholic mode of worship from its inception. That spirit has an agenda. The agenda in question is to obfuscate the Holiness of the Godhead in heaven—the Father, Son and Holy Spirit, respectively. That spirit is making the age-long attempt to splice the Virgin Mary, a mere mortal, into the Godhead and reshuffle the same. In doing so, that spirit works the brains and the hearts of all Catholics to pray to the Virgin Mary. By praying to her, they are of the assumption that she will entreat her son Jesus on their behalf for the answer to their prayers. This foregoing earthly sentiment sounds nice to some of us. After all, shouldn't we honor our mothers, too? How much more the honor we ought to bestow the mother of all mothers: the mother of our savior—the Virgin Mary.

Well, nice as that might sound, the Catholics are forgetting something. They are forgetting that such earthly sentiment in relation to the Virgin Mary does not hold in the kingdom of God. The kingdom of God, using the instrument of the Ten Commandments, has made known its eternal laws to us in the bible. In one place, the Commandment says, "Thou shall have no other gods before me." In another place it also says, "Thou shall not make for yourself any carved image—any likeness of anything that is in heaven above or in the earth beneath or that is in the water under the earth. You shall not bow to them nor serve them. For I the Lord your God; am a jealous God; visiting the iniquity of the fathers upon the children to the third and fourth generations of those who hate me"

Therefore, it is now clear that the Catholic problem is indeed lawlessness. They blatantly demonstrate their lawlessness in their denominational worship practices. Given the supreme laws of the Almighty God above, you can see the overt violations by the Catholics on the second, third, and fourth of the Ten Commandments.

Therefore, the Catholic religion clearly falls short in jurisprudence with regards to the kingdom of God. They cannot worship God in an open view of clench-fisted disobedience and still be pleasing to Him. Besides, these laws were given long before the Virgin Mary was even born in Israel.

Further, the Christian Bible clearly shows that the Virgin Mary has no part, will never have any part and does not belong to the Godhead. Not even our Lord Jesus Christ deified His sweet righteous mother. Not even James the other son of the Virgin Mary, the blood brother of Jesus, deified his mother. In all his writings in the book of James, there is no place where one can see their mother deified.

In the gospel scriptures, it is written that Jesus is the way, the truth and the life. He is the only one in all of eternity who can entreat the Father on our behalf. The gospel corroborates this fact. From the gospel of John 14: 13-14 Jesus says, "And whatever you ask in my name, that I will do, that the Father may be glorified in the Son."

Also in chapter 15:7 you will find the following: "If you abide in me and my words abide in you, you will ask what you desire, and it shall be done for you." Therefore, you should know now that the spirit that dragged the Virgin Mary into the affairs of the Godhead is about lies. Hence, that spirit is not of God.

Now, let's enter into the world of the Jehovah's Witness denomination. For starters, the name of their group falsely indicates they worship the heavenly Father. Assuming we join them in their folly, we will then embrace a doctrine that strips down the Godhead in heaven. Unlike the Catholics, who actually add the Virgin Mary to the Godhead thus increasing the size, the Jehovah's Witness remove the Son entirely from the Godhead and pay no attention to the Holy Spirit at all. In short, they go the great length of altering the Christian bible so that their particular doctrine may be fully disseminated. As a result, the Jehovah's Witness' bible omits 1 John 5:7 that says, "For there are three that bear witness in heaven: the Father, the Word, and the Holy Spirit; and these three are one." Also, their doctrine forbids them to pray with others for fear that such prayers could be done in Jesus name, and they cannot stand taking that risk.

Therefore, for one to actually weigh in on their liturgy, it becomes necessary to perform the Christian spiritual litmus test on the Jehovah's Witness doctrine. Should one really embark on it, the results of the litmus test will not be blue and red as usual. Meaning, the color blue should represent blue skies denoting a happy day while the color red should represent the precious blood of Jesus for the remissions of sins, liturgically speaking. Instead, you will be seeing black, which represents darkness. Meaning, there is no light in this religion. This is spiritually true seeing that they've taken diligent and meticulous steps to remove Jesus from their faith. In Christianity, Jesus is the light of the world.

Trailing this grave mishap of the Jehovah's Witnesses, it becomes easy to track and discern the agenda of the spirit that worked in the brain and the heart of the founder during its inception.

On the one hand, the spirit's agenda was to use the founder's ignorance of the Holy Scriptures against him and to bring to open shame his utter inability to rightly divide the word of truth and apply the same. On the other hand, the dark spirit triggered the founder's rush to capitalize on the gullible minds of his followers. In doing so, he would then vehemently lead a huge majority of human beings in a direction opposite from God.

At this juncture, I'd like to thank God for the coming of the Holy Spirit from the kingdom of God. His coming meant that the world cannot be deceived for long.

His mission is to take the things of Christ and declare them to us the Christians. To demonstrate His faithfulness, He has taken me through the scriptures. He has rightly divided the word of truth to me.

He is the Spirit of truth. He has shown me the boundaries that separate the Old from the New Testament. My ministry is therefore to share the truth with you His people all over the world.

Here is the truth: Jehovah is not God. Jehovah is really one of the archangels in heaven. Jehovah is in the same profile of angels the likes of Michael and Gabriel. The following bullets serve to illustrate how they have served God and humanity:

- Archangel Michael fought the war that broke out in heaven against Lucifer that brought his fall from heaven to the earth. That fall turned Lucifer to Satan and his angels to demons... (Rev.12:7, Isaiah 14:12- 17)

- Archangel Jehovah was the one who appeared to the patriarchs—Abraham, Isaac, and Jacob during their notable encounters in the scriptures of the Old...(Gen.12:1, 17:1-10)

- Archangel Jehovah was the one who appeared to Moses in the phenomenon of fire in the burning bush. He was the one who guided Moses and the Israelites out of the land of Egypt...(Exodus 6:3, Exodus 3:2)

- Archangels Michael and Gabriel fought against the evil throne of the prince of Persia who spiritually resisted as well as obstructed prayers and brought the answer for prayers from God to Daniel...(Daniel 10:12-13)

- Archangel Michael rebuked Satan on Mt. Nebo for trying to obstruct Michael's retrieval of Moses' body, which was then taken, not to heaven yet, but to paradise...(Jude 1:9)

- Archangel Gabriel appeared to John the Baptist father, Zacharias while burning incense and serving in the temple...(Luke 1:11- 19)

- Archangel Gabriel appeared to the Virgin Mary informing her about baby Jesus in her womb...(Luke 1:26)

- Archangel Gabriel appeared to the shepherds on a hill telling them of the birth of Jesus in Bethlehem...(Luke 2:8-14)

For your sound Bible knowledge, all these archangels are also known as Lords due to their rank in heaven. This is why the archangel Jehovah upon appearing to Moses and declaring his own name was referred to as the Lord God thereafter throughout the scripture. This absolutely takes nothing away from our Lord Jesus Christ. He is known as the Lord of Lords and the King of Kings in heaven.

As a bishop after the heart of the Father and Jesus Christ, I welcome your curiosity in wanting to prove that Jehovah is not God. He is not our heavenly Father. To start, you need to open your bible to John 5:37 and hear Jesus declare: "And the Father Himself who sent me has testified of me. You have neither heard His voice at any time nor seen His form." Meaning, the Jews who thought that Moses heard from God the Father in the wilderness were all wrong.

Should you want to know just how wrong the Jews were, then go back to when Moses first had the encounter on Mt. Horeb at Midian while tending the flock of Jethro his father in-law. The Old Testament scripture (Exodus 3:2) unfolds the story in this way: "And the Angel of the Lord appeared to him in a flame of fire from the midst of a bush. So he looked..." This means, it was truly an actual angel whom Moses saw as it is written.

Then in (Exodus 6:3) the original King James Version, that angel also known as Lord spoke the following to Moses: "I appeared to Abraham, to Isaac, and to Jacob as God almighty, but by my own name **Jehovah** I was not known to them." Meaning, he has appeared to the patriarchs as herein mentioned. Also, he carries the authority of God almighty as a messenger from heaven. However, to you Moses, I have a name and my own name is Jehovah. Right here in the Exodus writings are the words of Jesus in John 5:37 confirmed.

Then again, in Acts 7:30 and verse 53, the gospel lends more credence to this fact for you and I to believe. Most especially, beginning from verse 51 and ending in verse 53 the gospel states: "You stiff-necked and uncircumcised in heart and ears! You always resist the Holy Spirit; as your fathers did, so do you. Which of the prophets did your fathers not persecute? And they killed those who foretold the coming of the Just One, of whom you now have become the betrayers and murderers, **who have received the law by direction of angels** and not kept it."

48

Right here, the truth of what transpired during the ministry of Moses is made clear before our eyes now. The gospel did not stop here. It went on confirming this truth also in the book of Hebrews chapter 2 verses 1 through verse 3.

Now that the truth is well known, I implore all churches in Christendom to hallow our heavenly Father. We all must address Him by His true name: Abba Father. We should never again call Him Jehovah.

We should remember, any time we call Jehovah, we are worshiping an angel. We ought to know that worshiping angels is indeed a spiritual taboo especially in the kingdom of God. See Revelations 19:10, 22:8-9.

In my heart of hearts, I am of the belief that as you read this particularly peculiar book of mine you are indeed thinking as a wise thinker. In your thoughts, you are able to sort out all the mess currently besetting human beings both in the secular world and in the ecclesiastical domain. In either of the two cases, there is one central problem connecting them—the cunning spirit of lies. Lest we forget, notice that the agenda remains the same. The agenda of the evil spirit is to adamantly, with sinister schemes, supplant any truth with lies relative to the issue or circumstance in question.

Is there any more reason you should wonder why Charles Darwin promulgated the evolution theory? There is no other reason save for the scheme to supplant and drown the truth of creation.

Is there any more reason you should wonder why Adolf Hitler sponsored the makings of the Arian race? There is no other reason save for the scheme to nullify the diversity of human beings on the face of the earth. Therefore, the morbid idea in anyone or a group to make one race superior to all others is indicative of the lying spirit at work.

That is why the legacy of the late Dr. Martin Luther King Jr. lives on. Although it was riddled with overt racism amid other atrocities leveled against African Americans by the whites, his legacy was built on the solid rock of truth: The American Constitution.

The truth that all men are created equal and are endowed with certain inalienable rights became the joy that enabled him to endure the cross. Armed with the truth, he saw through the lies masking segregation, mob-lynching, cold-blooded murders and so forth. He knew these were sinister schemes deployed by the wicked spirit in white folks to rob African American people of their rights and equality as fellow Americans.

In fighting back the white powers of that day, his rebuttal was on two distinct fronts. On the first front, he persuaded the black community to maintain a policy of non-violence. On the second front, he relied unequivocally on the letters and the spirit of the great American Constitution.

It is there that the truth of what it is to be an American is told. Therefore, no matter how many times he was put in jail for this cause, he did not flinch nor buckle under. No matter what lies were paraded in his face, it was still insufficient to serve as a deterrent. The truth as entrenched in the Constitution proved much more powerful in his brilliant mind.

Forty years later, after the cold-blooded murder of Dr. Martin Luther King Jr., the United States voted in and inaugurated their first African American President. On January 20th, 2009 President Barak Obama took oath of office and moved into the

White House. This particular reality serves as a pivot of hope for all of us. There is hope that we can overcome the spirit of lies with the spirit of truth. All we need, just like Dr. King, is a thorough knowledge of the truth and perseverance.

That, my dear friend, is the essence of this book. It is the nucleus of the coming of the Son of God bringing salvation through the gospel. It is the mortar and the brick stone given for the building of the kingdom of God here on the earth as it is in heaven. It is the battle between the spirit of truth and the spirit of lies. Above all, it is the huge scale of joy we stand to experience when truth conquers lies after the long battle.

So the Kingdom State of existence means that humanity as a whole receives and retains the spirit of truth on the inside. Hence, as living temples, we have just the spirit of truth harnessing and developing our brains, hearts and sensory organs producing all manner of good.

This is exactly what Jesus Christ, who is our perfect model, meant (John 14:30) when he said to the disciples, "I will no longer talk much with you, for the ruler of this world is coming, and he has nothing in me." Spiritually speaking, Jesus implied here that there was an encroaching spirit on the horizon.

That encroaching spirit had no good intentions. Therefore, He, Jesus Christ must cease from talking. Also, that spirit has nothing in Jesus.

The spiritual implication of the above statement is clear to us. Jesus Christ is the embodiment of a person living the actual kingdom state of existence experience. During His human life here on earth, Jesus had one spirit on the inside: The Holy Spirit—the spirit of truth—the spirit of His Father. All His vital organs: the brain, the heart and sensory organs were in perfect working order. So when He said for the ruler of this world is coming, and he has nothing in me, He meant that the truth inside of Him cannot be polluted since the spirit of lies—the ruler of this world is unable to get inside his body. Jesus perceived that lying spirit afar off before it would get much closer. His sensory organs were that sharp.

Let me ask you this poignant question. When was the last time you were able to sniff the presence of a bad spirit coming around? I am not asking you about having a premonition of something predictable as a pattern of our life experience on earth. You know, the usual Murphy's Law—anything that can go wrong, will go wrong—that we all say. I am talking here about you sniffing the spirit of lies working in the church.

Just like in any of the arenas previously discussed, the spirit of lies works the same way in the church. Its agenda is clear: to pollute the truth. The truth is that salvation is given to all mankind and is only available in the New Covenant—the gospel. The gospel is not symmetrical to the scriptures given to Moses about the time before or during his ministry. Certainly, the gospel is not in symmetry with scriptures given to any prophet of old—from Samuel to Malachi. But the spirit of lies stealthily gets potential Christians to imbibe the scriptures of the Old Testament instead of the gospel. In some cases, the spirit of lies gets churches that claim they are espousing Christianity to adamantly despise the scriptures on which Christianity is invariably anchored.

Obviously, the spirit of lies has blinded their minds so gravely they cannot understand the promise of Covenant changes, which was spoken of even in the old days by Prophet Jeremiah. In the days of Jeremiah (Jeremiah 31:31-34) the Spirit of the Lord spoke through him and said, "Behold the days are coming says the Lord, when I will make a new covenant with the house of Israel and with the house of Judah—not according to the covenant that I made with their fathers in the day that I took them by the hand to lead them out of the land of Egypt. My covenant, which they broke though I was a husband to them, says the Lord. But this is the covenant that I will make with the house of Israel after those days, says the Lord; I will put my law in their minds and write it on their hearts; and I will be their God and they shall be my people.

"No more shall every man teach his neighbor and every man his brother saying, 'Know the Lord' for they all shall know Me from the least of them to the greatest of them, says the Lord. For I will forgive their iniquity and their sin I will remember no more."

Howbeit that we the people of this our age and time to whom this new covenant was promised cannot receive it? Again, you can clearly sniff the presence of the spirit of lies at work in our minds to supplant the truth. It would interest you to know that Jeremiah and the people of that time were practicing the laws and the doctrine of Moses. They were not given the gospel. The gospel came in our time by Jesus Christ, two thousand years ago since Calvary.

Another style of Jesus in bringing on the gospel was about change in one's view on tithing. Meaning, the gospel has authoritatively replaced tithing with a new and righteous way, a way that is more pleasing to the Father, Son and Holy Spirit, a way that enables you to prove the righteousness of God in Christ Jesus is working in your mind and in your heart.

To prove that good, acceptable and perfect will of God, you must switch from tithing to *giving*. To that end, Jesus had to admonish the Jewish leaders saying, "Woe to you, Scribes and Pharisees, hypocrites! For you pay tithe of mint and anise and cumin and have neglected the weightier matters of the law: justice and mercy and faith. These you ought to have done without leaving the others undone." Given the admonition that you've just read, the falsity of tithing as a righteous sacrament practice in the church is exposed.

Firstly, like those blood of animals in the temple at that time, tithing never really pleased God. It displeased God, not as a practice, but for all that it was lacking as a matter of spiritual principle. Indeed, tithing, Jesus says, lacked justice and mercy and faith. In a nutshell, they are the building blocks of a relationship—human or otherwise. Therefore, the situation with tithes, from the scale of the admonition by Jesus, raises the question as to why it should even be observed any further by anyone. Christians want more than anything to please God by faith.

It is finally revealed in the gospel that the Jews of old had no direct relationship with the Father, Son and Holy Spirit (John 5:37-38). They were always, as per the law, operating under the direct auspices of a human high priest in the temple. Also, whatever they received as scriptures came not by the Son of God (as with the gospel) but through angels to them (Acts 7:30, 53).

It becomes clear that tithing could never yield blessings on the enormous scale as giving does. All that tithing lacks in principle under the law, giving provides a Christian believer. It is a new order from God to us by His own Son.

Giving is the begotten sacrament of love. Giving commensurate the resounding clear language of the gospel: for God so loved the world that He gave His only begotten Son… Giving puts a Christian believer in godly character and characteristics. I mean that when you give, you assume a godly role and exhibit godly characteristics.

In love, justice and mercy and faith are present. These are the causes for which love endorse, advocate and fight and even die. Since love is the epitome of God's righteousness, and giving is a begotten sacrament of love, it is clear then that giving is therefore is a sacrament, which epitomizes the righteousness of God. Since giving puts you in character with God, and God is love, then the practice of the sacrament of giving invokes in you love on two fronts: (1) the love of God, and (2) the love for God, respectively.

The Love of God in a Giver

This is the actual gift of the Son of God, Christ Jesus, dwelling in your heart. He dwells in your heart by His spirit. He is there because you have received Him as a gift from God. Not that you earned this gift. But that God the Father just decided to give. While in there, He replaces the unclean spirit (Matthew 12: 43-48), which has departed wandering about in dry places seeking rest. As the unclean spirit returns, it finds no more room in your heart because the Son of God has taken over His rightful temple. You belong to Jesus and not to the unclean spirit.

Contrary to the unclean spirit, the agenda of the Spirit of Christ in you is to download, like in a computer, the nature and the character of God through your brain into your heart. Tithing is the direct opposite. Being rolled over from Abraham into the law and the doctrines given to Moses, it was and still is a derivative of the law, which the Bible calls a schoolmaster. A schoolmaster is one with carnal sensibilities only. All he does is constantly whip people in the effort to bring them to order. These people never get it. As a result, the schoolmaster continues to whip them to order. Still their brains and their hearts remain in total disconnect from the order in question. In all, the entire whipping exercise is riddled with frustration, tears and cursing.

Christians do not need a schoolmaster. They have Christ dwelling on the inside. This is why the gospel says, "But you are not in the flesh but in the Spirit, if indeed the Spirit of God dwells in you. Now if anyone does not have the Spirit of Christ, he is not His" (Romans 8:9).

The spiritual implication here is clear. It means that you give because you are openly declaring by the act of giving, that the Spirit of Christ dwells in you. After all, you have acknowledged the biblical truth that Christ is indeed a gift given to you, and you have received Him. This act by God of giving Christ to the world has now taken root in your own heart and mind and is blossoming.

Conversely, the spiritual implication with tithing is also clear. You pay tithes because you are openly declaring, by the act of tithing, that the Spirit of Christ does not dwell in you. Remember that the person of old—the time of paying tithes in the man's built temples—the Spirit of God was not yet given to them. Therefore, they neither knew the ways of God nor knew the heart of the Father like a true Christian. Remember (John 14:6) Jesus is "the way, the truth and the life. No one comes to the Father except through me."

Since Jesus came into this world by the act of giving—as in John 3:16—then as a Christian worshipper, you ought to have now known the way and the heart of the Father.

Also, the gift of Christ is not for you at all as one who pays tithes, but for others. Further, this act by God of giving Christ to the world does not take root in your own heart and mind and is not blossoming. Meaning, you are really not a Christian.

Now, given the broad analysis so far on tithing, can you detect the spirit that is behind it? You will agree with me that the spirit behind tithing is the spirit of lies. Its agenda is to obfuscate the gospel truth pertaining to Christianity. That gospel truth is the act of giving. In essence, it is seeking, and has succeeded in some cases, to supplant the following gospel truth for which giving is the operative language:

- "Now hope does not disappoint, because the love of God has been poured out into our hearts by the Holy Spirit, who was given to us. But God demonstrates His own love towards us, in that while we were still sinners, Christ died for us" (Romans 5:5-8).

- "There are diversities of gifts, but the same Spirit...But the manifestation of the Spirit is given to each one for the profit of all; for to one is given the word of wisdom through the Spirit...." (1 Cor. 12:4-11).

- "His divine power has given to us all things that pertain to life and godliness through the knowledge of Him who called us by glory and virtue, by which have been given to us exceedingly great and precious promises, that through these you may be partakers of the divine nature..."
(2 Peter 1:3-4).

Giving is to Christianity what breathing is to life. The love of God to us is clearly demonstrated through His acts of giving. He gave us His Son—the Word. He gave us His Spirit along with the gifts of the Spirit. God did these things to bring us into his divine nature. He did these things in order to induce the love for God in us. Jesus never paid tithes nor approved of it. Tithes lack justice and mercy and faith.

The Love for God in a Giver

The love for God in a giver is the sincere effort by a person exemplifying the divine nature of God in Christ Jesus. After receiving all that the love of God has brought to life, one now seeks to reciprocate to God. Meaning, the love of God now triggers the love for God in a Christian——as the saying goes: we love Him because He first loved us. You have also heard: blood in blood out. Or, love in love out. But how can you really show God your love? And by what means can your love be shed abroad God's own heart too like His in yours?

The answer is simple. Do exactly like He has done: Give! It is one of the eternal gospel commands and shall remain an everlasting commandment of God. To demonstrate this, Jesus (Luke 6:38) therefore declares, "Give and it will be given to you; good measure, pressed down, shaken together and running over will men put into your bosom. For with the same measure that you use, it will be measured back to you." Being that you say you are indeed a Christian, can you see now that giving is to Christianity what tithing was to Judaism? Moreover the two practices cannot be mixed at anytime. Those are the words of Christ, which He says repeatedly that they are not His, but the Father's who sent Him.

Precisely, giving inherently provides the checks and balance scales that keep heaven and earth in harmony. On the one hand, a person maintains a faith-based vertical reporting relationship to God. This is possible simply because you give from the heart and your conscience bears witness on the inside that you indeed do partake of the righteousness of God.

On the other hand, a person sharpens his or her instincts showing mercy and rendering justice through the horizontal human-to-human interactions and accountability. Again, this is possible owing to the fact that the people you bless by giving are not judged by you as undeserving of your gifts regardless of their lifestyles. Hence, you show people mercy. Moreover, by giving, you help to replenish that which the enemy, using situations and circumstances, either stole or tried to prevent them from getting. Hence, through giving you show godly justice to people. A lot of times, when you give, it is in fact an answer to someone's prayer that day.

Giving enrolls you in the divine-human-network. Unbeknownst to many, humanity has, since the manhood of Jesus Christ, entered into divine arrangements. It is written in the gospel that by one man, the second Adam—Christ—righteousness has entered the world. Also, He became sin for us that we might become the righteousness of God in Him. So giving is indeed a divine act. It definitely promotes altruism in humanity.

It causes you to activate, stir up and equally tap the providential force field in the human universe. Through this force field, the alchemy of God's providence works miraculously to meet both your needs and that of others. This is analogous to the economic concept of supply and demand by Adam Smith. Accordingly, Adam Smith alluded to the fact of the invisible hands in the free market place arranging the supply and demand to produce equilibrium. In the same fashion, the Apostle Paul (2 Cor. 8:12-14) by the Holy Spirit says, "For if there is first a willing mind, it is accepted according to what one has, and not ac- cording to what he does not have. For I do not mean that others should be eased and you burdened; but by an equality that now at this time your abundance may supply their lack, that their abundance also may supply your lack—that there may be equality."

Certainly, giving should be carried out by apportionment. This is not my wise opinion at all. It is truly a divine recommendation by the gospel. Meaning, the gospel recommends how giving should be appropriated as illustrated below.

- Concerning Pastors and headship (1 Tim. 5:17-18) of the church, it is written: "Let the elders who rule well be counted worthy of double honor, especially those who labor in the word and doctrine. For the Scripture says, 'You shall not muzzle an ox while it treads out the grain,' and "The laborer is worthy of his wages." Most importantly, take note of what is written in 1 Cor. 9:7-11 for Pastoral care.

- Concerning Workers in ministry (1Thess. 5:12-13) in the church, it is written: "And we urge you brethren to recognize those who labor among you and are over you in the Lord and admonish you, and esteem them highly in love for their work's sake. Be at peace among yourselves."

- Concerning church care (1 Cor. 16:1-2) for the membership, it is written: "Now concerning the collection for the saints, as I have given orders to the churches of Galatia, so you must do also: On the first day of the week let each one of you lay something aside, storing up as he may prosper, that there be no collections when I come."

- Concerning church outreach (2 Cor. 9:5-10) to communities and nations, it is written: ...he who sows sparingly will also reap sparingly, and he who sows bountifully will also reap bountifully. So let each one give as he purposes in his heart, not grudgingly or of necessity; for God loves a cheerful giver...Now may He who supplies seed to the sower and bread for food supply and multiply the seed you have sown and increase the fruits of your righteousness."

Clearly, you can see, from the above gospel scriptures, both a faith- based vertical reporting relationship to God—for God loves a cheerful giver—and a horizontal human to human interactions and accountability—he who sows sparingly will also reap sparingly, and he who sows bountifully will also reap bountifully. In practice, you will find that giving makes mercy and justice sing a life song. Therefore, a Christian is indeed his brother's and sister's keeper.

Misplaced Piety for a Misplaced Priesthood

Inasmuch as you have read up on how to compare and contrast giving versus tithing so far, there still could be room for inadvertent apostasy. Perhaps, you are not fully convinced yet whether you should follow the gospel way and give or drawback to the Law of Moses and continue to pay tithes. But before you drawback, I'd like to crave your indulgence for just a little while longer. I'd like to have the honor of sharing with you the knowledge revealing how the spirit of lies tried to make everyone err.

That knowledge is this: The spirit of lies caused Christians to show misplaced piety for a misplaced Priesthood. Simply put, the spirit of lies, just like in the secular world, twisted the minds of Pastors and members of the church to view Christ, on whom their salvation is anchored, as Levi—one of the grandsons of Abraham—that cannot save humanity. Christ is indeed greater than Levi. Christ has saved the world by His death and resurrection. Further, there is a Priesthood Order pertaining to each one by God in heaven.

To Levi, there is the Levitical Priesthood. To Christ, there is the Melchizedek Priesthood. Invariably, one is indeed greater than the other. Can you tell which one?

The Melchizedek Priesthood is for the New Testament worshiper. Christians are under the Melchizedek Priesthood. The Levitical Priesthood is for the Old Testament worshiper. Our beloved, non-Christian Jews are under the Levitical Priesthood. Christ as the Son of God installed and initialized the New Covenant, which is Christianity. Moses as a servant of God installed the Old Covenant, which is Judaism. Christianity came by the blood of Jesus Christ through the writ of the gospel scriptures. Judaism came through Moses by the writ of the Laws

61

and commandments sealed with the blood of animals. In practice, Christianity and Judaism do not mix.

Judaism as a religion of the Jews excludes outsiders, who are not of the same genealogy. Judaism is tribally and traditionally regulated and observed. You cannot become a Jew by mere confession or taking a liking to Jewish culture. You become a Jew by birth. You have to literally be of the same blood line. By blood line, I mean, that of Abraham by virtue of Isaac, the son of promise to Abraham, and not Ishmael.

In contrast, Christianity as a way of eternal life in God includes everyone who simply believes in Jesus Christ. This means even the Jews are invited and are welcome to the Christian faith.

With that in mind, you can see that the two separate priesthoods cannot be observed simultaneously together. You cannot observe the Levitical Priesthood while you are under the Melchizedek or Christ's Priesthood and vice versa. To do so is to commit a sacrilegious offense punishable by death.

This is the premise on which Jesus Christ was killed by death on the cross by His own people, the Jews. To them, at that time of the formative stages of Christianity, Jesus was tampering and was viewed as one in breach of their religious laws. Meanwhile, He was actually installing and initializing a new priesthood order—The Melchizedek Priesthood.

This is the priesthood under which Christianity is heavenly regulated. Unlike the Levitical Priesthood where mortal men as high priests offered up animal blood for atonement year after year, Christians have a High Priest after the order of Melchizedek who (1) offered up Himself (2) died and rose (3) passed through the heavens physically, and (3) is seated at the right hand of God.

Not understanding the difference between the two priesthoods has plunged many Christians into the grave spiritual mistake of practicing tithing. I believe that if these Christians understood the difference between the two priesthoods, the word *tithes* would not have entered into their vocabulary. Now that they are fully schooled on the subject, they are going to abstain from exhibiting misplaced piety for a misplaced priesthood by paying tithes. Indeed, tithes and tithing are perpetually synonymous with the Levitical Priesthood. Neither Christians nor Christianity is regulated by the Levitical Priesthood.

The Biblical Annulment/Abolition of Tithes

You have gained the knowledge to rid yourself of the artificial guilt imposed on you to pay tithes by your church. You now can ascertain which priesthood you are under as a Christian. You now know that giving corresponds to Melchizedek Priesthood; whereas tithing corresponds to Levitical Priesthood, respectively. Christians honor Jesus Christ in their faith, and not Levi.

Knowing that you cannot mix the two in practice, are you going to let a man or a woman of God intimidate you into violating the covenants? Jesus knowing the tricks of the spirit of lies spoke, concerning the future of Christianity, saying that one cannot take a piece of a new garment and attach it to the old. Fast forward to now, you can see the relevance. The agenda of the spirit of lies is to take just one aspect of the Levitical Priesthood—tithes—and toss it in with Christian sacraments of worship.

Was Jesus smart or what? I mean, He laid it out then just as we see it now before our eyes. Jesus saw way beyond the cross what the spirit of lies was up to. That spirit kept sneaking up on Him and the disciples.

For example, when Jesus had just finished telling the disciples that He must go to Jerusalem and He be killed by the chief Priest and elders, Peter, meaning well, told Jesus not to say things like that. As a result, Jesus rebuked Peter saying, "Get thee behind me Satan..." meaning, Satan is the master mind behind the spirit of lies.

Jesus knew that Satan would come and confuse Christians, by using other Christians, not to show their piety for the right priesthood. Jesus knew Satan would cause Gentiles in worship to start acting like Jews. Or better yet, Satan would make Gentiles think by espousing the Jewish traditions they could gain enormous access to heaven. After all, Jesus is a Jew. Well, as surreal as that might sound to you, it is highly misplaced.

To demonstrate this point in context, open your bible to Hebrews Chapter 7. Trail with me the spiritual argument on tithes eloquently presented here by the gospel. The first thing you will notice is the mentioning of the two priesthoods: The Melchizedek and the Levitical. The second thing you will notice, especially in verse 7, is that the Levitical Priesthood is lesser; whereas, the Melchizedek Priesthood is better. Hence, in the context of the biblical argument, the lesser is blessed by the better. Do you want to know why that is the case?

Accordingly, verses one through six enable you to ascertain the origins of tithes. It began with Abraham. He gave a tenth of the spoils of war to Melchizedek, king of Salem, upon returning from the slaughter of kings. Abraham was not a Jew. He was a Chaldean. However, the God who made heaven and earth called him and promised to make a new nation of people through him. Abraham was a pagan worshiper when God interrupted his paganism and called him out from amongst his kindred folks. Therefore, having no godly laws yet nor a church to guide him, Abraham maintained certain humane aspects of his pagan customs. One of such customs of the Chaldeans was tithes.

Giving a tenth of the spoils of the war to Melchizedek, priest of the Most High God, was significant on the part of Abraham. It was so significant that it was incorporated into the laws of Moses for the Jews to observe. In observing the law on tithes, the other eleven tribes paid it to the tribe of Levi, who served in the temple as priests. However, as a law, the sons of Levi tribe were exempt in the sense that they received instead of paying tithes. The bible states that their exemption is directly attributed to what Abraham did with Melchizedek.

Therefore, that act of Abraham towards Melchizedek, priest of the Most High God, resulted in the installation of a Jewish priesthood—Levitical Priesthood. To that end, the bible (Hebrews 7:4-6) states, "Now consider how great this man was, to whom even the patriarch Abraham gave a tenth of the spoils. And indeed, those who are of the sons of Levi, who receive the priesthood, have a commandment to receive tithes from the people according to the law, that is from their brethren, though they have come from the loins of Abraham; but he whose genealogy is not derived from them received tithes from Abraham and blessed him who had the promises."

It simply means that the act of Abraham towards the Priest of the Most High God was before any promise that God made him ever manifested. He neither had Ishmael nor Isaac yet. However, God was so delighted in Abraham over the act that God rewarded him by choosing a priesthood to serve God from Abraham's great grandchildren. At this time of the act, his great grandchildren existed only in posterity.

For you to understand the length, width, depth and the height of how God qualified and reconciled the act, the bible again (Hebrews 7:8-10) states, "Here mortal men receive tithes, but there he receives them, of whom it is witnessed that he lives. Even Levi who receives tithes paid tithes through Abraham, so to speak, for he was still in the loins of his father when Melchizedek met him." Meaning, you ought not to misconstrue the prefix: Here mortal men receive tithes. It only implies the Levitical Priesthood by verbiage. It does not pertain to Christianity in any way shape or form. Also, you ought not to misconstrue the suffix: but there he receives them, of whom it is witnessed that he lives. It speaks only of the place where Abraham met with Melchizedek and performed the act.

For your understanding, God promised Abraham at old age something he never had all through his youthful years. And that was the promise of a son by Sarah his wife. This was something that seemed impossible in the natural. With this promise in his heart, Abraham encountered Melchizedek, Priest of the Most High God while returning from war. During the encounter, he gave a tenth of the spoils from the war to Melchizedek. In doing so, he received a blessing. The blessing was priestly in nature. It implies here that God intended, with the same promise of a son to Abraham, to make worship an inextricable part of the posterity.

Abraham did not know that at the time. He was only showing his obeisance to the king of Salem as it was customary in his pagan experience. It is retrospectively similar to the story of Adam and Eve. Adam never held the thought that it was not good for him to be alone.

God was the one who said that. Then God put Adam in a deep sleep. Took one of Adam's ribs and formed Eve. Adam never knew that Eve whom he was to have and hold was already inside of him yet unformed. Only God knew all of that.

Likewise, Christians in Christ Jesus have a promise from God. This is something that no one on the face of the earth ever had, not even Adam and Eve.

To this end, the gospel states, "he who believes in the Son of God has the witness in himself; he who does not believe God has made Him a liar, because he has not believed the testimony that God has given of His Son. And this is the testimony: that God has given us eternal life, and this life is in His Son. He who has the Son has life; he who does not have the Son of God does not have life" (1 John 5:10-12).

Just like Abraham who needed to have a son to fulfill his earthly manhood and to produce God-oriented posterity, so is all humanity in need of ageless existence to live and fulfill each individual destiny.

With that in mind, let's take a closer look at Melchizedek. From the gospel the following is read, "For this Melchizedek, king of Salem, priest of the Most High God, who met Abraham returning from the slaughter of kings and blessed him, to whom also Abraham gave a tenth part of all, first being translated *king of righteousness* and then also king of Salem, meaning *king of peace,* without father, without mother, without genealogy, having neither beginning of days nor end of life, but made like the Son of God, remains a priest continually" (Hebrews 7:1-3).

To me, I say this man was and is deep. Considering the fact that Melchizedek remains a priest continually having neither beginning of days nor end of life, the blessing he gave Abraham was however measured and limited in scope. He being made like the Son of God did not impart to Abraham or those in his loins all the quality of life Jesus is known for.

Even though they had the Levitical Priesthood, Israel as a whole broke the covenant God gave them through Moses. But Jesus whose priesthood is after the order of Melchizedek kept all the commandments of His Father resulting in the whole world having a new covenant.

With the breaking of the old covenant, the Jews rendered imperfect the Levitical Priesthood. They could not be perfected observing any ordinance, tithes included, under their priesthood worship. This is why the gospel states, "therefore if perfection were through the Levitical priesthood (for under it the people received the law), what further need was there that another priest should rise according to the order of Melchizedek, and not be called according to the order of Aaron? For the priesthood being changed, of necessity there is also a change in the law." Meaning, as tithing was a law through Moses to the Jews (under the Levitical priesthood), so also is giving a law by Christ to Christians who are under the Melchizedek priesthood. Starting from verse 13 the gospel continues on saying, "For He of whom these things are spoken belongs to another tribe, from which no man has officiated at the altar. For it is evident that our Lord arose from Judah, of which tribe Moses spoke nothing concerning priesthood. And it is yet far more evident if in the likeness of Melchizedek, there arises another priest who has come, not according to the law of fleshly commandment, but according to the power of an endless life"   (Hebrews 7:11-16).

Jesus has come to perfect our faith in God through the instrument of the gospel. With the gospel, He taught new ways of relating to God and relating to one another. Amongst His teachings all across Mathew Chapters 5 through 7 you will find the words: "Therefore ye shall be perfect just as your Father in heaven is perfect." This means, perfection of worshipers of God is inevitably entrenched under the Melchizedek priesthood.

Abraham, on the other hand, relied on and followed his cultural instincts when he gave just a tenth part of the spoils of the war to Melchizedek. As you do the math, you will quickly come to the conclusion that if he only gave a tenth part, then he had more in his possession from the war. But he could not think beyond just the tenth part. He was just culturally and traditionally impacted and perhaps a bit stifled. He did not have the Holy Spirit inside of him to help and guide him on how to perfectly worship God. That was the reality of life then.

This reality permeated every aspect of the promise Abraham received as it became real and manifested as in the children of Israel. From Isaac, the main son of the promise to Jacob and then the twelve sons of Jacob, the nation of Israel worshiped God through the direct auspices of their culture and tra- ditions. This was inherently passed down to them from their great grandfather, Abraham. Therefore, as tithes and tithing became part of their laws, it was still a throwback affair. It lacked the Spirit of God in it. It lacked the nature and the quality of life of God in it. As Jesus puts it, he says, it lacks justice, mercy and faith.

Therefore, it is safe for me to posit that Abraham's faith was rather limited in scope for someone we all refer to as the father of faith. It was limited to him believing God for the promise of a son. It never tied in his personal nature of being as a man. He believed God for a son to the extent that he never went about sacrificing to pagan gods for it. Given the time, the age and the way of life then, demonstrating his belief in the Most High God qualified him as a friend of God.

However, there were other dimensions relative to Abraham's personality that needed perfecting. One such dimension is having complete trust and reliance on God's providence. Simply put, he did not know he could trust God to provide. As a result, he only gave a tenth part of the spoil to Melchizedek.

In the Old Testament Abraham's descendants struggled with this issue of trust in God for forty years in the wilderness. Their constant murmurings and agitations in relation to any challenge resulting from their lack of trust in God led to the biggest mistake of Moses. Having not received the Spirit of God on the inside, their carnal-mindedness was at odds with God. Hence, a change for a second and better covenant was in order.

We thank the Most High God for sending Jesus Christ, whose mind and nature of being are in perfect harmony with the Father. From and through Him, we Christians have the mind of Christ. With this mind, we use it to trust God and rely on His providence. Hence, the gospel lends more credence to our belief as it says, "And it is yet far more evident if in the likeness of Melchizedek, there arises another priest who has come, not according to the law of fleshly commandment, but according to the power of an endless life"

To accomplish this, God put forth the following words in the holy bible: "For on the one hand there is an annulling of the former commandment because of its weakness and un-profitableness, for the law made nothing perfect; on the other hand, there is the bringing in of a better hope through which we draw near to God....by so much more Jesus has become a surety of a better covenant. Also, there were many priests, because they were prevented by death from continuing. But He, because He continues forever, has an unchangeable priesthood" (Hebrews 7:18-24).

In Jesus, you will find that the dichotomy of faith has its relative balance easy for the mind to decipher. As a Priest after the order of Melchizedek, Jesus died to fulfill the old covenant requirements as a consequence of its breach by the Jews, and He rose (on the third day) to establish the new covenant all in Himself. Hence, He continues forever.

The narratives I have given you so far make up the biblical annulment or abolition of tithes. As you notice, the bible presents the annulment on two critical fronts. On the one front, tithing is biblically annulled by the change in priesthood through Levi (Judaism) to the priesthood through Melchizedek (Christianity).

On another front, tithing is abolished by a change in covenant—from the old (Genesis thru Malachi) to the new (Matthew thru Revelation). Accordingly, our faith as Christians, is perfected by the scriptures entrenched in Matthew through Revelations.

Trading Places, Trading Priesthoods

Although Paul the Apostle, as a Pharisee, totally converted from Judaism to Christianity, his story speaks for a Jew embracing a covenant change. Under the Law of Moses, Pharisees were not Priests. As a result, they could not serve dispensing the sacramental Jewish rites in the temple. This, by the way, was strictly reserved for the Levites.

In those days, Levites were, by the Law of Moses, the recipients of tithes. To them as well as the rest of the Israelites, the law was the final authority for their way of life. They saw their receipt or collection of tithes from their brethren as their God-given right. As a result, it was strictly enforced by them. Anyone amongst the Jews that sought to deviate was severely punished accordingly. Therefore, Levites, being highly revered by the Israelites, could not afford to show any sign of apostasy. This bedrock of loyalty to their ordinance of tithes made the Levitical priesthood strong and unshakeable.

But who would have imagined when the Holy Spirit came as in Pentecost that something so unique would occur that resulted in trading places and trading priesthood by a Levite. Accordingly, the gospel in Acts 4:36-37 says, "And Joses, who was also named Barnabas by the apostles (which is translated son of en-couragement), a Levite of the country of Cyprus, having land, sold it and brought the money and laid it at the apostles' feet."

Wait just a minute here. Can you see here that a Levite, whose life, by their religious laws, was to receive tithes from his people, has now switched sides? As you can clearly see, in his noble move to switch sides, he did not pay a portion of his proceeds—as in tithes. Rather, he joined in on a phenomenon borne out of a different priesthood order—the Melchizedek priesthood. Ladies and gentlemen, this Levite, joined in on the new phenomenon called giving. In doing so, the bible tells us—having land, he sold it and brought the money and laid it at the apostles' feet. Meaning, he gave all the proceeds to the apostles like the other Christians. He did not give a tenth part.

As a thinking person, two things flew out of my mind after reading this gospel scripture. On the one hand, it shows that our beloved Jews can become Christians. It is the new and living way. The adage that salvation is of the Jews is strictly in the idea that Jesus Christ is indeed a Jew because of his earthly maternal link to the Virgin Mary. But salvation is for all people on the face of the earth, who believe in Christ Jesus and are born again, being filled with the Holy Spirit.

On the other hand, it gives me more impetus to nail my final argument on tithing as a spiritual, ugly misfit in Christianity. In trading places and trading priesthoods, this Levite has become, in my book, the epitome of the great ideal that Christianity is indeed progressive. It does not go backwards into the things of old. By following Jesus Christ of Nazareth, every Jew and Gentile believer moves forward from the natural to the spiritual things of God, and does not remain in a rut. God is indeed a Spirit.

As a progressive ideal, the kingdom of God or heavenly order is for all that believe (Jews included) to become Christians. It is not for Christians, who, having believed, now to regress into Judaism. For one thing, such Christians cannot qualify as Jews simply because it is only earned by being born as one into the Jewish earthly bloodline. Hence, Gentiles can never be Jews naturally speaking. If you say you are a Jew spiritually, then it means you have obtained the circumcision of the heart. In this context of our discourse, you should not be practicing tithes and tithing in your church. Doing so would mean you do not honor Christ but Levi. And Levi is not at the right hand of the Father in heaven. Jesus is.

Most importantly, since a Levite has broken ranks with his Levitical priesthood and has practiced giving, then you, a Gentile, a Christian, have no excuse whatsoever to revert to tithes. With this book, God is calling forth all your Christian instincts and sensibilities to come out from within you. To this end, the gospel reveals to us (Rev. 2:8-9) how Jesus really feels about any such apostasy—"and to the angel of the church in Smyrna write, these things says the First and the Last, who was dead and came to life: I know your works, tribulation, and poverty (but you are rich); and I know the blasphemy of those who say they are Jews and are not, but are a synagogue of Satan." Therefore, I, the Bishop, ac- cording to the New Covenant life implore you to honor the Melchizedek priesthood with giving, in which your Christianity is conducted.

Chapter Seven

The Scrutiny of Christianity

Our Lord Jesus says that no one comes to Him except our heavenly Father draws him or her. The thought of one being drawn by God almighty to His dear Son is rather deep. It means that the Father is closely watching your every move. He is watching what you do with His only begotten Son. He is watching what you do to His only begotten Son.

Analogous to these impressions of our heavenly Father in one's mind are the lyrics to the famous tune by the '80s duo named Hall & Oats. The song is titled "Private Eye." It is something along this line: "…private eye. I'm watching you. Watching your every move. O, oh, private eye…." Perhaps, it is more closely linked to the lyrics by the '90s British group named the Police. Penned by my man Sting, the song "Every Breath You Take" tops it for me. Most especially, I like the climax of the song: "…oh can you see you belong to me. My poor heart aches with every move you make…" You are apt to agree with me after listening to that, the song is a perfect fit. Indeed, we belong to the Father.

Written by these talented songwriters and artists, these songs serve to guide as well as guard our relationships. In the case of "Every Breath You Take" Sting covered a majority of the core values— 'every vow you break' –necessary in one's ability to foster rock solid commitment in a relationship. This is exactly what the Father in heaven is watching to see. Therefore, for this cause, the gospel by the words of Jesus (John 4:23) declares, "But the hour is coming and now is, when the true worshipers will worship the Father in spirit and in truth; for the Father is seeking such to worship Him." And so the Father watches on and on…

Watching What You Do with His Son

In this aspect, with unfeigned respect to our heavenly Father, there is only one inference to be drawn in your mind. Simply put, you are viewed by the Father as being friends with Jesus Christ, and not just a servant. "No longer do I call you servants, for a servant does not know what his master is doing; but I have called you friends, for all things that I heard from My Father I have made known to you"
(John 15:15).

Being friends with Jesus is higher in ranking than the kind Abraham enjoyed. For one thing, Jesus is the lamb, which Abraham told Isaac that God will provide for Himself for a burnt offering. For that reason, the angel Jehovah prevented Abraham from killing Isaac as a burnt offering to God. Instead, angel Jehovah pointed to Abraham a ram caught in a thicket. The blood of Isaac was not perfect for the remission of sins of the whole world. It is only the blood of Jesus Christ.

This was already set up from the foundation of the world. Long before Abraham would even be born. This episode of using Isaac was merely a test. God was testing Abraham's heart. Indeed, he was being weaned of child and human sacrifice, which were common in paganism from which he was called. Hence, Abraham passed the test. But beyond all of these, I'd like you to recall that Abraham did not have any direct conversation with our heavenly Father. Only Jesus does. He is in the Father, and the Father is in Him. As a result, being friends with Jesus brings one into the centerfold presence of the Godhead.

The spirit of wisdom and revelation in the knowledge of Christ richly abound in you. Hence, you possess the uncanny ability to differentiate the anointing pertaining to the two testaments of the bible. In doing so, you understand that, in terms of anointing, the consecration of the writings of the first testament pertained, in its entirety, to finding a ransom for sin that entered the world through the first Adam.

That story in the Garden of Eden is summed up to what I call "Bite the fruit and swallow a devil." You would recall that nothing changed in Eve until she actually took a bite out of the fruit from the tree of knowledge of good and evil. Consequently, she took her gaze away from God, whom she had completely relied on for life and living, and placed it on herself. When Adam returned, the serpent did not have to tempt him anymore. Eve did the devil's bidding on Adam. They both fell from liberty of life. They plunged into bondage of sin.

Being friends with Jesus lets you see Him as that ransom given by the Father for the sins of the whole world. In that sense, you totally acknowledge Him as the propitiation for sin. In doing so, you understand that, in terms of anointing, the consecration of the writings of the second testament pertain, in its entirety, to life, liberty and the pursuit of the kingdom of God and His righteousness. With much confidence, your whole orientation is ordered in the manner that corresponds to the law of the spirit of life in Christ Jesus.

Being friends with Jesus gives you the impetus to take ownership of the foregoing gospel scriptures:

There is therefore now no condemnation to those who are in Christ Jesus, who do not walk according to the flesh but according to the Spirit. For the law of the Spirit of life in Christ Jesus has made me free from the law of sin and death…So then those who are in the flesh cannot please God…And if Christ is in you, the body is dead because of sin, but the Spirit is life because of righteousness. But if the Spirit of Him who raised Jesus from the dead dwells in you, He who raised

Christ from the dead will also give life to your mortal bodies through His Spirit who dwells in you" (Romans 8:1-11).

The Spirit teaches you how the first part works. Your body is dead because of sin if Christ is in you means the death of Jesus on the cross is accounted unto you through the taking of the Communion. With the Communion, you eat the bread and drink the wine of the sacraments. Symbolically, with the bread, you eat up His body as a burnt offering for not only your sins, but also for the sins of others you come in contact with everyday. Symbolically, with the wine, you drink up His precious holy blood that wipes away every imprint left by sin not only in your soul, but also in the soul of others you come in contact with everyday.

Holding onto these thoughts in your heart and mind every waking hour of your day causes regeneration to take effect by the Spirit of Christ in you. Consequently, since you know good and well that you have escaped condemnation, then you take all the necessary steps never to condemn others around you. Therefore, you make every effort to forgive all people, who do you wrong since you hold on to the belief that Jesus has forgiven you your mistakes. That is the spiritual meaning of taking Communion in church or home.

Being friends with Jesus, you know that by observing the sacrament of Communion, you affirm the righteousness of God in Christ Jesus. Further, you exemplify the standards of the golden rule. You personally do unto others as you would have them do unto you. Your obedience to live by the law of the Spirit of life in Christ Jesus is making your world a better place. In turn, you conquer the snare of the sin of unbelief: unforgiveness.

Being friends with Jesus allows you to come to grips with how much of a negative impact unforgiveness had in your life. For starters, it kept you in a state of being critical and judgmental of people you spent time with. Nothing they did would please you. You would always find fault with them. You saw nothing good in them. There was no future for these people in your mind. You were constantly remembering their past misdeeds done against you. And you held it against them forever. The sound of that person's name, the guilty one of all, was irksome to your mind. You wished you two had never met.

Given the fact that Christ in you allows you to catch the before and after difference of being friends with Jesus, you can discern what spirit was making you show an ugly side of yourself to the world. You know now that it was Satan all along.

The gospel says the devil is the accuser of the brethren. But now, the two of you have parted ways. And now, your life is unfolding along the line of the words, "...therefore, if you bring your gift to the altar and there remember that your brother has something against you, leave your gift there before the altar and go your way. First be reconciled to your brother, and then come and offer your gift" (Matthew 5: 23-24).

Therefore, it means you cannot be rightly related to God unless you are rightly related to the people close to you on a daily basis. This is not only important to you, but also true. As a gospel truth, the bible says, "And this commandment we have from Him: that he who loves God must love his brother also" (1 John 4:21).

Being friends with Jesus brings you to gain greater insight into the deeper meaning of the following words:

> I beseech you therefore brethren, by the mercies of God, that you present your bodies a living sacrifice,

holy, acceptable to God, which is your reasonable service. And do not be conformed to this world but be transformed by the renewing of your mind, that you may prove what is that good and acceptable and perfect will of God" (Romans 12:1-2).

Let me put your mind on a rewind mode. Let's revisit the art of presenting your body or (bodies) acceptable to God, which is your reasonable service. Remember that through the law of sin and death—the Law of Moses—Israel had many virgins in the land. With the abundance of virgins, Mary found favor with God. In her virgin body, there deep inside her womb, God planted the holy seed that was Jesus Christ. Giving birth to the Word in the flesh was indeed Mary's reasonable service to God.

Let me put your mind on a fast-forward mode. Since the resurrection and ascension of Jesus Christ into heaven, the Holy Spirit has come to the world. As a result, you and I now possess what Mary did not. Even though she kept Jesus in her womb, she was not filled with the Holy Spirit, yet. The child in her was filled. She finally received the Holy Spirit on the day of Pentecost along with the others in Jerusalem. She was amongst the 120 that day. If she was filled already then she would not have been with them in the upper room waiting and praying. In fact, she was there with the rest of the brothers of Jesus—James, Joses, Judas and Simon.

Likewise, your body, like Mary's, through the law of the spirit of life is slated to carry the Spirit of the Son of God, which is your reasonable service. Being not conformed to this world you are transformed by the renewing of your mind through your daily efforts of soaking in the gospel scriptures from Mathew to Revelation. In doing so, you read one chapter a day from each book of the gospel.

By this exercise, you spiritually brainwash yourself. The gospel scriptures take hold of your mind replacing doubts with faith. They replace fear with power. They replace confusion with clear thinking and focus. They replace anxiety with trust and patience. They replace anger and frustration with hope. They replace depression with love and joy. These negative experiences came from the world into you.

Lack of reading, praying and sometimes fasting on account of your word knowledge resulted in these negative experiences taking root in your mind. In taking root, they became strongholds that torment a person. Torment is never the will of God for you. Victory is indeed the will. Your victory plan is set in three phases: the good, the acceptable, and the perfect will.

The Good Will

You, like no other creature in God's creation, was made totally in the image and likeness of God, meaning, your physiology is just the right fit for God's presence and apropos to the eternal plan and overall concept of life. To this end, the apostle Paul (1Cor. 6:19-20) says, "Or do you not know that your body is the temple of the Holy Spirit who is in you, whom you have from God, and you are not your own? For you were bought at a price; therefore glorify God in your body and in your spirit, which are God's." So by opening up to the message from a preacher and accepting Jesus Christ as your Lord and Savior, it becomes your first step in proving that good will of God. By accepting Jesus as your Lord, you are now presenting your body a living sacrifice.

The Acceptable Will

At this juncture, you start to talk the talk and walk the walk. To accomplish this, you locate where in the bible the earthly life and time of Jesus is written. Discover how He lived in Jerusalem,

Nazareth, Judea, Tyre and Sidon, Capernaum, Galilee and so forth. Check out His thought patterns and characteristics. Notice how He interacted with people on a daily basis. Notice how He always gave honor to His Father in heaven. Study His teachings such as the beatitudes. Pay great attention to how He broke the Laws of Moses and replaced them with the new and living way—the Christian way.

Study His parables and get their meaning. Try to find the correlation between the parables of Jesus and your personal life experience. Do not live your Christian life in breach of the covenants. Maintain your Christian priesthood, which is the Melchizedek priesthood.

With regards to your finances, strictly observe your Melchizedek rule. Meaning, you give, and not tithe. Watch and pray that you are not cajoled by a preacher into paying tithes thus violating your priesthood. With love, pass on the knowledge of the priesthood change to the preacher and the church.

Take Communion as a true Christian and not like someone still under the Laws of Moses. Go beyond the outward water baptism to the inward baptism of the Holy Spirit and fire. Go beyond the outward, fleshly circumcision to the inward circumcision of your heart by the Spirit of God. Possess the Christian will to deduce from meditations that faith, beyond all controversies, is not something randomized, but synchronized. It is indeed synchronized to flow in accordance with the will of the Father.

Take for instance, the case of the man (John 9:1-5) who was born blind. The disciples wanted to know, given the gravity of his blindness, if it resulted from his sins or that of his parents. But Jesus told them, "Neither this man nor his parents sinned, but that the works of God should be revealed in him..." Invariably, if it is true in this case, then it is true in all others. By staying immersed in the doctrine of Christ, you are now proving the acceptable will of God.

The Perfect Will

Understanding the perfect will of God has become somewhat elusive for Christians. For this reason, a huge majority put their energy on things that do not matter and neglect the weightier matters of the faith.

To help you get a hold of it, let me start by telling you what it is not. It is not casting out devils. Although it does help a great deal to clear the way for His perfect will. If it were true, then the Lord (Matthew 7: 21-23) would not have made the following expressions: "Not everyone who says to Me, 'Lord, Lord,' shall enter the kingdom of heaven, but he who does the will of my Father in heaven. Many will say to me in that day, Lord, Lord, have we not prophesied in your name, cast out demons in your name, and done many wonders in your name? And then I will declare to them, 'I never knew you; depart from Me you who practice lawlessness.'"

Many Christian fellows have founded their ministries solely on this premise. In doing so, they think they have scored high marks with God. At the end of the day, all they have succeeded in doing is to revel in and relish the power of God. They've only just scratched the surface, so to speak. After all, Satan does cast out Satan in the kingdom of darkness. That is really nothing new.

Even the Pharisees and Scribes (Luke 11:14-23) accused Jesus of casting out a devil with the authority of Beelzebub.

Signs and wonders are indeed phenomena in and of themselves. Both the kingdom of God and the kingdom of Satan perform them. That is why you do not seek after signs and wonders. You might be in for a trick or treat by a sorcerer the likes of Simon of Samaria. To get fully acquainted with that story, I'd like you to read Acts 8:9-24. Do not seek after a prophet for prophecy. You are therefore liable to be deceived. Chances are, your prophet of interest may not be in total harmony with the Lord Jesus Christ.

Without any further ado, the perfect will of God (John 17:3) is revealed by these words: "And this is eternal life that they may know You, the only true God, and Jesus Christ whom you have sent." Did you catch it when Jesus hinted at it above? That was the hint when he said—I never knew you; depart from me... Coming as lightening flash to Paul the apostle, he wrote about it, as his deep, personal desire to the Philippians church. In his (Philippians 3:10) epistle, he stated his heartfelt desire—that I may know Him and the power of His resurrection and the fellowship of His sufferings, being conformed to His death.

The revelation of the perfect will of God came when Jesus entered the final hours before the cross at Calvary. In this solemn, yet poignant moment at the garden of Gethsemane, Jesus reflected intently on all that had taken place within 3 years since His ministry began. If he must die, then it should be for a worthy cause. If his death was going to save us, then it wouldn't be so that we continue to live and mind our own individual careers, jobs and businesses, not giving one another any troubles at all. Or, that we spread out into our respective denominations and disseminate our differing and diverse creeds and doctrines.

Unlike monarchs and presidents of nations of the earth who, for safety reasons and fear of death, shield themselves from their subjects, God is the opposite. In sending Jesus to come and save us, His intention is that Jesus brings us into a face-to-face presence with the Father. That is why Jesus told us—blessed are the pure in heart, for they shall see God.

God lives forever. To see Him, we need a new, immortal body. This translates into us having eternal life. That life is in Christ Jesus. Once any of us makes it to the presence of God the Father, such a one will live solely and purposefully to really know Him, who is the only true God.

Our heavenly Father dwells in secrecy now. But He longs and yearns for us to get to know Him. Jesus in keeping with this same (Luke 10:22) eternal plan intimated—all things have been delivered to Me by My Father, and no one knows who the Son is except the Father; and who the Father is except the Son, and the one to whom the Son wills to reveal Him. Therefore, in the book of Revelations chapter 4, the apostle John, while on the island of Patmos had the enviable privilege of catching a glimpse of His outward physiology. Can you even imagine just how glorious the Father must look?

Now, if you have been in any kind of a relationship, you would know that it takes more than physical appearance to really know a person. You've got to get past mere platonic associations to the intimate level of dealings with the person. A wise black woman once said that to know a man just means you've got to cook for him. That is to say, a way to a man's heart is through his stomach, and not the mouth. Meaning, the eaten food does not stay in the mouth. It stays in the stomach. What went with the food to the stomach is the essence of the woman that cooked it. Honey, if the food tasted real good, in his mind, he sees her, and the food is secondary. In his quiet time of thoughts, he says she is definitely a keeper.

To see the plan that all humanity gets to know Him—the only true God—come to fruition, God rolled out a series of events in the world. The Father did these things in the effort to combat the artificial challenge posed by the spirit of lies (Satan) attempting to obliterate, in the minds of all people in the world, the fact that the only true God exists. As a matter of fact the way of the artificial challenge, the spirit of lies or Satan confuses the minds of the people to worship any and every thing in creation except the creator.

For instance, the spirit of lies makes some worship a cow. Some worship the moon. Some worship the things in the river and the ocean waters. Some worship man-sized molten images of bronze, gold, silver or brass. Some worship trees. Some worship demon spirits of ancestors. Some worship monkeys and the like. Some worship human authority figures. Some worship snakes.

Some worship huge stone figures. With humanity in such a shambled state, knowledge of the only true God remained a void. To fill the void, God did something unique and splendid in humanity. God created a new and improved breed of human being to keep the knowledge of the only true God alive.

The Divine Role of Jews on Earth

Have you ever wondered why the Jews are such a special people in the human race? Did you stop for a minute and think of the central reason Adolf Hitler wanted to exterminate them from the face of the earth?

The answer to these questions lies in the same reason they came into existence from out of the human race. A human race was largely steeped in polytheism, for your information.

Their existence, I say, can be likened to the blessing of innovation, which yields a new and improved product from the same old one we've had. It is truly and solely on that premise alone that the

Jewish people are special on the face of the earth. Therefore, beyond all controversies, including, but not limited to politics and religion, it is their natural existence that the knowledge of the only true God has remained here on this earth.

It would interest you to know that long before God would send His only begotten Son, Jesus Christ, to save the world, He had to create a race of people first whose orientation was in knowing that there is one true God above all other gods in this world. Also, beyond having the knowledge of the only true God, their orientation was in knowing how to worship Him as well. In short, the Jews were the only race of people in the entire human race, for the record, to have practiced monotheism.

To achieve this goal, God intercepted the idolatrous way of life of a certain man and called him out from the land of Mesopotamia. In the call, God asked him to depart far away from his kindred folks to a different place altogether. Along the way in this journey, God changed his name from Abram to Abraham and his wife's name from Sarai to Sarah. And at this point, the innovation began, spiritually, so to speak.

God made Abraham a promise that seemed humanly impossible. God promised him a son to be born from his wife who had aged past child-bearing years. When the promise finally came to pass, the household of Abraham enjoyed two sons: Ishmael first, afterwards, Isaac. Ishmael was by a slave girl named Hagar. Isaac was by Sarah, the true wife of Abraham. Now, the two children were different. What separates them is the same thing that serves to establish how special the one is over the other.

As a slave girl, Ishmael's mother, Hagar, was young and of course was of child-bearing age like any young lady. Therefore, her involvement to couple with Abraham had a natural predictable outcome. In many cultures of the world, especially in the African culture, old men marry real young ladies for the same reasons. Hence, the baby was not the one God promised Abraham. God keeps His promises.

With Sarah, however, she was old past child-bearing years. As a result, the birth of Isaac was indeed a human phenomenon. It was naturally impossible. Sarah was ninety years old when she had Isaac. That fact alone serves to establish just how special Isaac was compared to Ishmael. Since Isaac came by the miracle of God, then it was fitting for God to continue working His plan through the line of Isaac. Accordingly, Isaac begot Jacob. Jacob begot his twelve children. From these twelve children, we have the twelve tribes of Israel called Jews.

As a nation of people, they made sure the knowledge of the one true God was not lost in the earth. Because of them, other nations around them, the likes of the Egyptians, were shaken up and they took notice. Given the fact that the plan was working in the world, God decided to perfect it.

In doing so, God moved to get humanity past just having a glimpse of Him in their minds to knowing His heart and character. In other words, God decided to up the ante. To accomplish this, God sent His only begotten Son, Jesus Christ, to the world through the Jewish race and people. Only this time, God changed the religious dynamism. The promise of the birth of Jesus came through a virgin in Israel. With the birth of Jesus, the knowledge of the only true God entered a paradigm shift.

Immediately He was born, the spirit of lies that deceived the world that the one true God does not exist went into a rampage. In the rampage, the spirit of lies went into Herod and he killed every male child less than 5 years of age in the land. This Herod did in the effort to exterminate the boy Jesus. Consequently, Jesus and His earthly parents escaped to Egypt and took refuge there until Herod died. It was that same spirit of lies in Herod that also went into Adolf Hitler making him hate the Jews. Jesus later returned to Israel to complete His heavenly Father's mission on the earth.

Given this much insight in relation to the Jewish people, it leaves one with one solid impression. It leaves one to think of them as the physical, natural human obstacle to the sinister schemes of the spirit of lies moving about in the world.

The main agenda of the spirit of lies is to foil, if not downright obliterate, the chances of humanity knowing and worshiping the only one true God on the earth. So no one with his or her belief in this same one true God of the universe would even think of hating the Jews. Such a one or a group would have seen Jews for exactly who they are: the earthly essence of God's presence. Or even better, they would have seen the Jews as the human, personified intuitiveness of God to squash Satan.

Watching What You Do to His Son

The phrase as written above carries a distressing connotation. It seems to suggest that you are on the wrong side of things with God in relation to His Son, Jesus Christ. It seems to suggest also that you have neither learned the doctrine of Jesus Christ nor received Him as your high priest after the order of Melchizedek.

You are among those who put the works of the Law of Moses over and above, as if to deny, the works of Jesus on the cross at Calvary. Therefore, your action begs the question: Are you a Christian or an Israelite? As a Gentile believer in Christ, have you forgotten so quickly already that the Israelites were the first to be called into Christianity? Call into remembrance the fact that the twelve disciples of Jesus Christ were Jews, His own brethren in Jerusalem. I'd like you to call to your mind the fact that everything Jesus taught in the New Testament that make up the synoptic gospel were to the Jews first.

Mathew, Mark, (except Luke) and John were all Jews. These men wrote the first four books of the doctrine of Jesus Christ. In short, they wrote the first books on Christianity. Beyond them, we now have the likes of Paul the apostle, a Jew of the sect of the Pharisee, who brought the good news of the gospel of Jesus Christ to the gentile world. In his apostolic ministry all around the gentile world, Apostle Paul advocated strict adherence to the doctrine of Jesus Christ. To demonstrate his deep commitment to the doctrine of Christ, Apostle Paul admonished the Galatians church saying, "But even if we, or an angel from heaven, preach any other gospel to you than what we have preached to you, let him be accursed"   (Galatians 1:8-16).

As a deterrent, it targets those holding positions of authority in the church to curb any creeping sense of apostasy in relation to the doctrine of Jesus Christ on their part. If you are a Pastor or a leader of sort, I have just one question to ask you: were you called as a Jew into the ministry of the kingdom of God or were you called as a gentile believer? Your sincere, heartfelt answer to this question will help clarify things. Ultimately, your answer will drop you down from the fence to land squarely, on your two feet, on the correct side of your true calling.

The irony here is that the message above was from a Christian Jewish person to a gentile Christian church in Galatia. You cannot forget that fact. Therefore, if as its stands, Jews who have converted to Christianity boldly make the above declarations to us gentiles, what is any gentile person doing trying to propagate Judaism as a Christian? To preach any other gospel to young believers than what Jesus Himself as well as the apostle Paul delivered constitute you doing something **to** the Son of God. Definitely, cajoling your Christian church members to pay tithes constitute you doing something **to** the Son of God.

Compelling your Christian church members to take Communion while your sermons are buried in the reading of the Old Testament scriptures constitute you doing something **to** the Son of God. The bible says there is a veil that lies across one's heart at the reading of the Old Testament. Are you wiser than God that puts the veil there because of His Son and the superiority of the new doctrine?

The Father is definitely watching what you do **to** His Son. He has the following word for the likes of you: "For if we sin willfully after we have received the knowledge of the truth, there no longer remains a sacrifice for sins, but a certain fearful expectation of judgment and fiery indignation which will devour the adversaries. Anyone who has rejected Moses' law dies without mercy on the testimony of two or three witnesses. Of how much worse punishment do you suppose will be thought worthy who has trampled the Son of God underfoot, counted the blood of the covenant by which he was sanctified a common thing, and insulted the Spirit of grace? For we know Him who said, 'Vengeance is Mine, I will repay,' says the Lord. And again, 'The Lord will judge His people.' It is a fearful thing to fall into the hands of the living God"   (Hebrews 10:26-31).

Perhaps, you have carried on for so long in your ministry that it never faced you there is a problem with it in the Father's watchful eyes. Perhaps, the way you run your ministry is in symmetry to the so-called godly advice and approval of your mentors in the body of Christ. Perhaps, you are simply em- ulating your peers in the ministry business. After all, from all indications, they seem to be doing just fine. They seem to have money and are never too broke, come to think of it. Perhaps, being loud towards or snarling at your congregation in the effort to bid them to pay tithes, you are in keeping with what's in vogue.

Whatever your reasons are, under the Father's watchful eyes, they culminate to three distinct violations such as:

1. Trampling the Son of God underfoot,

2. Counting the blood of the covenant by which you were sanctified a common thing,

3. Insulting the Spirit of grace.

As you can tell, these violations are not my own opinions by a long shot. Indeed, they are what the kingdom of God says you are doing **to** the Son of God. If you must be made aware, it is a direct attack on the Son of God by you. Your ignorance or wanton ill- will is in fact counter-intuitive to the essence of the gospel of Jesus Christ.

The bible is candid in profiling culprits of these violations within the Christian faith. If you turn with me to the book of 1 Timothy 6 starting from verse 3 it says: "…if anyone teaches otherwise and does not consent to wholesome words, even the words of our Lord Jesus Christ, and to the doctrine which accords with godliness, he is proud, knowing nothing, but is obsessed with disputes and arguments over words from which come envy, strife, reviling, evil suspicions, useless wrangling of men of corrupt minds and destitute of the truth, who suppose that godliness is a means of gain." Do you fit this profile as a minister of the word?

I implore you to search your heart and let your conscience bear you witness for your innocence or guilt. If you are innocent, then walk before the Father and be blameless. But if you are guilty, then you must now learn your lessons and understand how and why you ended up committing these spiritually egregious offenses well-noted above. Continuing on from verse 9 it says: "but those who desire to be rich fall into temptation and a snare and into many foolish and harmful lusts which drown men in destruction and perdition. For the love of money is a root of all kinds of evil, for which some have strayed from the faith in their greediness, and pierced themselves through with many sorrows."

That's how you strayed from the faith. You fell into temptation triggered by your desire to be financially well off to say the least. The tempter of the brethren as you already know is Satan— the spirit of lies. But the way of escape has already been paved for you. Starting from verse 11 it says: "…but you, O man of God, flee these things and pursue righteousness, godliness, faith, love, patience, gentleness…."

Being repentant of heart and mind to the ever-watchful Father, no longer shall you ask your flock for their tithes again. As you can see now, it is a serious offense to Jesus and the Father. Ask your flock to simply give. Let your pure faith in Christ Jesus who gave the commandment on giving; prove to you that He is able to (1) work in them both to will and to do for His good pleasure, and (2) do exceedingly abundantly above all that you ask or think according to the power that works in you, meaning stay in the doctrine of Jesus Christ and you will increase in power. This is my spiritual dictum to you.

Chapter Eight

The Christianity Advantage

If you take a good look around the world, on any given day of the week, especially on Sundays, you will find hundreds of thousands or even millions of people showing piety to the objects in which they stake their faith. Whether or not these objects of their worship can actually breathe thus qualifying as a living thing, is of no consequence to their personal attachment to and belief in them. What really matters to them the most is the fact that they are able to satisfy that deep-seated human hunger on the inside to worship.

Worship is a human reality. We just can't help ourselves. Like food for the stomach, so is worship for the human soul. Even the atheists among us maintain a peculiar regiment of life that translates into them focusing more on themselves and relying on themselves. That too, is indeed a form of worship. In the case of the atheist, it is really the worship of the individual self. Being therefore a human reality, worship, like the air we breathe, the foods we eat, the sex we have, the positions of office we hold, the schools we attend and the education we receive, the families we build, the politics we play, the friendships we form, the enemies we make and so forth, should be about something. We should have purpose.

The English dictionary has several definitions for the word *purpose*. One dictionary defines *purpose* as: the reason for which something exists, or is done, made. That definition raises a question in my innocent human mind in relation to worship.

In my person, as the author of this book, I have lived long enough in this world. I have gone through the rigors as well as the rigmarole of daily survival. I know good and well that life in general is riddled with complexities. I have lots of issues and questions inside of me. I also have lots of issues and questions outside and around me. Situations and events break out in this world that leave me puzzled and outright frightened.

Every day of my life, these situations and circumstances seem to blow up and form mushroom clouds that cover my mind that I cannot see past the problems. I need answers to these questions. I need solutions to these problems looming in the world today. Are you just like me?

Since food is for the stomach as worship is for the human soul, then if I must bow down to anything, the purpose should be about:

- Getting answers to these life questions

- Finding solutions to these life problems

Satisfying my innate human need to worship should never increase the severity of these life problems. It should never leave me in bitterness. It should never lead me into planning and plotting violence. It should never push me to commit acts of violence against those not sharing my beliefs and faith.

If we ascribe names to and deify the things we worship, then our individual pious dispositions should never cause you to pit your god against mine. What I really mean is, seeing all the different things we worship in the world, it would be fool- hardy of you to pit your cow god against my lion god. You know one will eat up the other. Or, to pit the moon god against a sculptured image god. Since the two cannot speak nor mutter a sound, it means the moon god will only shine moonlight that floods the face of the sculptured image god. In the end, the moon god will simply rotate away on its axis. You guessed right, nothing really happened there.

Therefore, seeing the idiocy in relation to the worship of these lower forms of deities, I now come to the place where I must psychoanalyze myself. I must make sure whatever I bow down to worship is indeed not lower but higher than my intellect and everything in creation put together.

Beyond that, I want my deity not to be too different from me to where there is a total disconnect in any particulars cogent to us forming a God and man or woman relationship. Compared to me, my God should possess exponentially every trait, characteristics, and quality I possess to the extent that all of mine remains just a tiny speck.

That's who I want to call my God. The overall implication is clear. I move to start a relationship with my God with certain built-in guaranties. Since my God is a lot like me, He is most certainly going to know more about the issues and problems I face. Invariably, He has made provisions that can undergird me in all the areas I fall short. Simply put, my God holds the solutions to my problems and the answers to my questions in this life. Therefore, to bow down and worship Him is in translation a benchmark for the end of my quest for truth and peace in this world.

What you've just read is truly what Christianity is made of. Further, it is strictly on this premise that the advantage of Christianity lies in comparison to all other organized platforms of worship. Christians bow down and worship the God, who more than qualifies as the only true God of heaven and earth.

As a plus to all Christians, this God shares their image and likeness. The Christian bible records this truth in the book of Genesis 1:26-27. It says, "Then God said, 'Let us make man in our own image and likeness; let them have dominion over the fish of the sea, over the birds of the air, and over the cattle, over all the earth and over every creeping thing that creeps on the earth.' So God created man in His own image; in the image of God He created him; male and female He created them."

The word above signals an undeniable compatibility between us human beings and the God Christians bow down and worship. From the word, it is clear that there is absolutely no disconnect between us and this God in every aspect of our human experience. The operative word here is that He made us, and not us who made Him with our hands. In other words, we humans are a product of His imaginations, and not vice versa.

Further, He made us with a purpose. The purpose was for us to have dominion over cattle or cow, birds, fish, and over all the earth, and not vice versa. Therefore, the thought that human beings can stoop so low as to bow down and worship the likes of a cow and man-made objects is not only ludicrous, but absurd.

If this misplaced disposition of man strikes you as a problem, which it is in the world today, then you need to pay close attention to what the Christian bible gives as the root cause. The bible says this particular problem resulted from the fall of man in the Garden of Eden.

In the story, the fall of man was due to the cunningness of a deceiving spirit being which man was totally oblivious to. In the cunning game, the spirit lied to the woman first making her bite the fruit and swallow a devil. From that point on, all intellectual capacities of mankind were subject to the remote control of the spirit of lies and its corresponding manipulations.

For me to know that much makes all the difference as a thinking person. In life, I have found out that part of solving a problem is to first understand it. When you understand the problem, you can then trace it to its source. These wise words are a direct derivative of the schools of thought involving the sciences, engineering, medicine, economics, government and so forth.

It is definitely no different from the Christian approach to life. It allows me to find the correlation between the social upheavals in the world and the deceitful manipulations of the human minds just as during the fall. The results are seen in the form of corruption, betrayal, segregation, cheating, murder, lies, scandalous affairs, apostasy, greed, witchcraft, sorcery, nepotism, bribery, unnatural sensual affections, idolatry, hatred, anger, foul language, irresponsibility, poor judgments, fallacies, myths, gluttony, tribalism, sectarianism and so forth. The effects of these reverberate across the domain of politics, the economy, religion and business. It just seems like there is no end in sight to these problems in the world.

Looking to ourselves for solutions as humans has proven futile to say the least. The best of our noble efforts has been the proliferation of prison facilities for criminals in our respective societies and nations. But even the penitentiary confinement seems to better serve the interest of the crime itself than it does to reform and transform the criminal. Therefore, the prisons are not the perfect solutions. However, the removal of these criminals away from the mainstreams of society for a time and time cannot be overemphasized. What still remains is everyone in the world taking a closer look together and checking out the philosophy that lends more credence to the facts and reality of our human issues.

It's time we turn a new page. It's time we stop grappling with these problems the same old fashion way. Another wise saying that we all have is this: The law of insanity is doing the same thing over and over, but expecting a different result. By keeping our focus just in the United States alone for example, we can catch, prosecute and jail a Charles Keating for emerging to defraud seniors of their life savings, but it did not prevent Bernard Madoff from committing securities and investment fraud in Wall Street. We can expose and scandalize a Jimmy Swaggart for falling from grace by having sex with a prostitute as a preacher; it never stopped a Ted Haggard from having unnatural affection towards another man also as a preacher.

In other parts of the world, we have their governments dispense justice for crimes to include, but not limited to stadium beheadings, hangings, and grindings as one would a piece of meat in a grinder, which is a more sinister way to die. Since there seem to remain a continuum, then this continuum serves to alert everyone and equally begs the question: Whose interest do these killings serve? Obviously, the citizenry cannot seem to stop asking for these punishments by committing crimes. So does the government kill them all and therefore solve crime problems finally? Or does the government realize that its people are the resource that rejuvenates and regenerates the system. I say, the people of any society are the lifeblood of that society. To kill them all is to kill off the society. Where do you stand?

When nations cannot balance this equation in life, they need not resort to religious indifference and make that a bone of contention. That is nothing more than a camouflage. It does not get rid of the problem on the ground. Creating a law such as the Sharia Law is indeed a fly on the wall to eavesdrop on the people and use their vulnerabilities to kill them. The only one that benefits from such a law is the one at the enforcing end. Should the role be reversed, he will be the first to seek absolution. He would suddenly realize that he is equally grappling with the same issues as the others he has oppressed. As a result, he would prefer a more humane treatment.

By expressing this view on Sharia law, I do not in any way shape of form endorse nor subscribe to hate. I cannot hate those who formulated the Sharia law. That would be un-Christian of me. On the one hand, I know that they are merely grappling with human problems from the outward symptoms perspective.

On the other hand, I know that if they were fully aware of what's behind the life or run's the life of a person on the inside, then they would take a different approach. They judge the outside where the symptoms are clearly seen. I see through to the inside then I judge a person. God sees the inside therefore He gave us Christianity.

All over the world, we face a human problem, and not a religious one. Religion has spawned more divisions than it has brought unity. The recent 9/11 disaster in New York that brought down the two World Trade Center Towers, serves as a prime example. In the disaster, thousands of people were murdered that day. It has become the crockpot of all sorts of debate. The Muslim extremists that were responsible for the disaster claim it was justifiably done against America, an infidel nation, meaning they can no longer sit and watch their Islamic nations get polluted by the American way of life.

Well, here is the missing thing. The American way of life is freedom, justice and liberty for all. If their people are drawn to it, then it simply suggests that their way of life is not conducive for their people.

When Americans complain, it is not to switch to Islam, but to correct any discrepancies with the American way and restore the same. America has laws that govern its people. These laws provide the checks and balances for Americans to live their lives. But here is the other missing thing. Neither the Islamic world nor the Freedom world of the Americans is crime free. How do we handle this particular fact of life itself?

Our religious differences can't save us. Our governments can't save us. Our tribes can't save us. Our universities can't save us. Our idolatries can't save us. So what or who can save us from our human woes and weaknesses? Let me remind you here that a huge majority of these white-collar criminals graduated from Ivy League citadels of higher learning. Michael Milken, the junk-bond man, is indeed a graduate of Harvard School of Business. It would be disingenuous of any of them to say they stand for the good of all people, considering their level of education unless each one of them has truly repented.

Since we cannot depend on ourselves to find solutions to these issues, we must therefore look beyond ourselves. I am glad for this hope that exists for humanity. I am glad that we never say "never" no matter the obstacles we face. When some of us said, "we cannot fly," some of us went into research and came back with airplanes. Today, we've made an industry out of flying. It has become a major source of employment globally. Careers have come out of the airline business for the betterment of our lives. We have even flown beyond planet earth. We have flown to the moon. How about that for finding a solution to our human problem?

Where we are today in relation to our human character flaws is no different. The good news is that we already have a solution. The solution is not natural. The solution is indeed spiritual, meaning we lack the right spirit on the inside of us to guide our thoughts and guide us into all goodness of life and living.

The reason we keep missing it is due to the fact of the spirit of lies that went inside Adam and Eve. When they ate that fruit, they swallowed a devil, short and simple. Since then, humanity and all our capacities have remained subservient to Satan.

Empirical data from medical science show that we are what we eat. Whatever nutritional values are contained in any given meal gets into your body when you eat it. What is in apple differs from orange, for example. Dr. Oz, in one of his television shows demonstrated how strawberries hold certain cleaning properties for the human dentition. In doing so, he called out a female guest from the audience. He made her stand with him. Together, they bit a few strawberries into their mouths. Afterwards, each used the index finger to brush the teeth with the bitten strawberries. When it ended, each one had a brighter dentition. The audience applauded with excitement.

In the same way, the fruit off the tree of the knowledge of good and evil was real. God who made the strawberries, apples and oranges made them all. The only difference was the fruit of that particular tree in the garden contained spiritual properties not suitable for human consumption. With obedience, man would have been able to escape the trickery and the manipulations of Satan. With obedience, man would have kept Satan on the outside looking in, and not inside looking out, as the reality is today. Also, you ought to know that Satan is a spirit being, while we humans are mere mortals. Our victory as humans over Satan is also in whom we listen to and what He gives us to eat and drink this time around.

On this premise enters the Christianity advantage again. This time we not only have an understanding of our problem, we have a gift to resolve the issues. We have the gift of the Son of God, Jesus Christ given to us by the only true God of life. Although He came through the Jewish line into the world, He was the only person born with a Spirit stronger than Satan on the inside. As a result, He defeated Satan in the wilderness when tempted for 40 days and nights. He is the reason the Christian faith exists as a New Testament called the gospel.

The holy bible has also the Old Testament. In it, the story of the fall of man as well as the ramifications that ensued through the years of time is meticulously documented. Overall, the Old Testament speaks to the fallen state of man and the victimization of humanity as a whole. However, it holds something else pertinent to the crime-free people we crave to become. It holds the promise of the gift of the Holy Spirit—Joel 2:28-32.

That promise was therefore fulfilled in the New Testament. Everything humanity stands to become is modeled out by Jesus Christ and the twelve disciples in the New Testament. Hence, the New Testament speaks for the rise of man from the fall and the fresh new possibilities now and beyond. That is Christianity, in essence.

If we all have the Spirit of Christ on the inside, then all our capacities will become rightly regulated. In turn, our unruly or ruthless behaviors become completely modified. My confidence in this truth is in the gospel. Study them for yourself and see. Jesus with the Holy Spirit inside of Him did not promulgate religious laws as you will find in the Old Testament. He broke the religious laws. He turned a new page. Those laws were unprofitable. They did not promote a healthy human-to- human relationship. Instead, He gave the world philosophies that speak for better living. Indeed, through these philosophies of Jesus we all get the proper handle on how to relate to the only true God.

For example, Jesus taught us saying, "You have heard that it was said, 'You shall love your neighbor and hate your enemy.' But I say to you, love your enemies, bless those who curse you, do good to those who hate you and pray for those who spitefully use you and persecute you"   (Matthew 6: 43).

From where I stand, I have yet to see any organized religion make such statements. I have yet to find a person willing to supplant his or her reckless religious laws with noble life-giving philosophies.

If we are willing to equally supplant our reckless religious laws with human friendly ones, then there wouldn't be future disasters the magnitude of 9/11. If we embrace Jesus Christ sincerely, then we will cease to see intelligent men use their intelligence only for greed and corruption. For this cause, Jesus taught us saying, "The lamp of the body is the eye. If therefore your eye is good, your whole body will be full of light. But if your eye is bad, your whole body will be full of darkness. If therefore the light that is in you is darkness, how great is that darkness" (Matthew 6: 22-23).

This is the truth of the teaching. Smart people or intelligent people in this world get that way by studying. To actually study, they use their eyes to read. The knowledge they gain is light inside of them. Therefore their whole body is full of light. However, what hangs on a balance is their motive with regards to that knowledge gained. The notion of motive serves to signal what manner of spirit dominates the person. It is the spirit that regulates how the eyes interpret what it takes in.

If the spirit in the person is Christ, then how that knowledge is applied will be good. If the spirit is Satan, then the knowledge when applied will only yield bad reports. However, there is a third level of knowledge acquisition here. If that knowledge that one gets is already couched in evil tidings like in the occult, then we have a major problem on our hands.

Who can forget the recent CNN television broadcast, which aired on September 9, 2010. This was one of Larry King Live special-interview sessions. It involved the world-famous Physicist and Author: Stephen Hawking. Was it not shocking to see the words of Jesus Christ above come to light before our own eyes?

In a poignant moment such as this one, the shock is never on the line that these lies of Satan still exist and count in the world today. To me, the shock is truly on the line that another human soul

103

has been manipulated on the inside just like Charles Darwin was. Again, the spirit of lies – Satan—lays hold of the faculties of a brilliant man (a Professor at Cambridge University, England) and attempts to obfuscate the truth. To accomplish this, Satan plants those seeds of lies in the brain of Stephen Hawking and his co-author. Together, they write a book entitled *The Grand Design*. Given the tone of the dialogue from the interview, the agenda of this book is clear to me. It is the age-old attempt of the spirit of lies to obliterate the knowledge of God in the universe, short and simple.

In the book, *The Grand Design*, Stephen Hawking controversially argue that God did not create the universe. Further, he maintains that science can explain the existence of the universe and the scientific account is complete. Therefore, theology is unnecessary.

We do not need to invoke God in order to explain the existence of the universe. Also, given the existence of gravity, the universe can and will create itself from nothing. Hence, spontaneous creation, he maintains, is the reason the universe and humanity exist.

This is the real world that you and I wake up to face each passing moment of our earthly lives. It is riddled with the constant battle of truth versus lies. It is riddled with the battle of light versus darkness. If what Stephen Hawking says were true, then human beings would be slithering like snakes out of the ground following the result of the gravity-compression effect. In fact, this ideal would make gays and lesbians happy indeed. Instead of having to face the ridicule or the cumbersome process of adoption, sperm donor and such, they would just wait for the cycle of the human popping act from the ground and take which gender they so choose.

The proponents of scientific laws and theories serving to supplant the truth of God as the creator of the universe will almost always applaud the literary work of Stephen Hawking contained in *The Grand Design*. However, the opponents of the lies of Satan will always lean on the person of the Holy Spirit and hear the still small voice of Christ on the inside telling them the following, which constitute my **Christian Philosophy of life** otherwise known as the **C-rule** concept:

> **Rule 1.** The spiritual philosophies of Jesus Christ or the C-rule concept pertains to the human frontier in the universe, which harnesses and incorporates into use all physical laws for its noble sustenance and humane existence.

> **Rule 2.** The laws of physics and all the sciences in the universe are regulated by and remain subject to the spiritual laws of Jesus Christ. It is the realm of the miraculous such as (1) the ascension of Christ into heaven against gravity, (2) the feeding of five thousand men with just five loaves and two fish, and (3) the miracle of the three Hebrew children not burnt in the fiery furnace.

> **Rule 3.** The universe in its current state exists to showcase the enormous demand factor inherent within itself and the distribution of the same to its inhabitants without sufficient supply. The supply is strictly a function of knowledge. As knowledge increases, so is the supply factor to meet the demand. The knowledge is a gift of the Holy Spirit.

> **Rule 4.** The nothingness that science purports we all come from in the universe exists to herald science's incompleteness of thought and the barrenness from hasty conclusions. The C-rule maintains that the nothingness is the mystery for which God is invoked consequent to

105

the completeness of thought and fertility from conclusion that the laws of the universe are not randomized but synchronized.

Rule 5. The synchronicity itself is the congruity of each species as a true reflection of the source of origin. Whether we are animals or humans, we reflect our parents in looks, character traits and DNA. Being humans, we reflect the heart of our heavenly Father and possess the mind of Christ. Our conscience is the benchmark of such encounter in life.

This is my Christian stand against the wiles of Satan consequent to the lies of Stephen Hawking in his book *The Grand Design*. My authority in the stand is found in the gospel as in 2 Corinthians 10: 3-5 that says, "For though we walk in the flesh, we do not war according to the flesh. For the weapons of our warfare are not carnal but mighty in God for pulling down strongholds, casting down arguments and every high thing that exalts itself against the knowledge of God, bringing every thought into captivity to the obedience of Christ…"

The authority so given in the gospel to all people signals your Christian advantage. As pertinent knowledge, it allows you to assume and maintain a winning position all the time in relation to the barrage of issues you face each day. If the weapons of warfare are not carnal as in guns and bullets or any object suitable to destroy others and lives, then you, by the alchemy of the gospel has entered into the realm of the spirit where Satan continues to hide. This is the secret advantage of Christianity above all others. In warfare, you do not destroy human lives. You go after Satan directly. You use weapons far superior to that of Satan. The Holy Spirit who is in you as a Christian gives you the weapons to fight.

With that in mind, I posit that Christianity is a perfect fit for the entire human race. It is not in the same league as the religions of this world. From its inception, it pulled far away from the religious laws of the Jews to establish itself as the new and living way.

Jesus had this to say about religious laws (Matthew 23: 4) and those that make them: "...for they bind heavy burdens hard to bear and lay them on men's shoulders; but they themselves will not move them with one of their fingers."

With the belief in Jesus Christ, one obtains salvation and enters a new-birth experience. With the impartation of the Holy Spirit, one starts to actualize his or her power over the real enemy of us all: Satan—the spirit of lies. The work is all done on the inside of a person. As a result, your brain, your heart, and all other faculties become rightly poised for good, and not evil. The benefits are enjoyed on the outside world by the person. Further, you become a good neighbor to your fellows worldwide.

Given my personal experience and triumphs in life under the faith, I reject the notion that Christianity should be lumped in with others and be called a religion. From the teachings of Jesus Christ, my conviction remains firm. I believe therefore I speak, saying—Christianity is not a religion, but a higher or spiritual philosophy of life. The English dictionary gives philosophy the following definitions: The rational investigation of the truths and principles of being, knowledge, or conduct. It is also a system of principles for guidance in practical affairs. Further, it is a calm or rational attitude. I totally agree.

All these definitions describe well the teachings of Jesus Christ. In truth, they simply tell the world the entire content of the gospel. The gospel tells the world the truth of how we should relate to the only true God of life and to one another. The life we share human to human is not at all fictional, but a practical affair. The gospel speaks of love for God and for each other. Love is the cure for our human woes. The laws of God through His Son, Jesus Christ are human friendly. They make up the entire gospel. The gospel is all that Christianity is built upon, and not on the Old Testament. Therefore, the gospel is the Christianity advantage.

References

Nelson, T. (1992). The Holy Bible. [New King James Version]. Republic of Korea: Thomas Nelson Bibles.

Random House. (2010).Webster's Dictionary Revised and Updated [4th ed] New York: Ballantine Books.

Hawking, S. (2010). Theology unnecessary, Stephen Hawking tells CNN [12 paragraphs]. Larry King Live – CNN. [On-line serial]. Available: Doc. No. 2779

Rancho Cucamonga,
CA. 91739 (909) 815-5635

E-mail: nseklloyd@gmail.com

Food for Your Thoughts

It is man who confused Christianity for the whole world. God did not. The confusion has remained strictly a function of the spirit in man, which has rendered the nature of man inapposite with respect to God's ways, heart and mindset.

Given that evil nature, man finds it virtually impossible to keep the Ten Commandments of God. Any effort by mankind to keep them is strictly a function of a different spirit in man. Humanity needs the spirit of Christ on the inside to live right. This reality is therefore the work of Jesus Christ in the world. This book is the divine approach to bring mankind into alignment with our Lord Jesus Christ. Our heavenly Father sees humanity as one entity indivisible and deserving of justice and liberty for all. Therefore, He sent His only begotten son, Jesus Christ, to come and be the answer to all our human questions of this life.

Is it a wonder to you that His ministry was never on the line of forming a new group or sect that would embark on some renegade religious agenda? If such were the case, it would have made Jesus Christ a traitor to God the Father, who sent Him. Instead, you are apt to find a catchphrase that is a common thread tying His mission together in a tapestry of love and unity. That catchphrase in question is the word "The World."

Have you read or heard how Jesus said, "I am the light of *the world*?" Perhaps, you read or have heard how Jesus said,"... go ye therefore into all *the world...* " Certainly, you must have read or heard this: "For God so loved *the world* that he gave His only begotten son that whosoever believes in Him should not perish but have everlasting life."

Therefore, Christianity should never be confined to exclusivity consequent to the masquerading religious denominations we have in the world today. This is the bedrock of the confusion, and it is indeed counter intuitive. The church of Jesus Christ is the entire world itself. Worship is to God what romance is to us, humans. It is a relationship on an intimate level. The Old Testament records the fall of man into sin with a corresponding lifestyle and the promise that man will surely rise again from the fall. The New Testament is a celebration of the rise of man from the fall through the person of Jesus Christ. Hence, the promise has been fulfilled. God's concentration is in the gospel where He infuses His nature into human nature thus transforming it.

That is why you can never ever mix the two Testaments in real worship to God. That is why the doctrine of Jesus Christ is Non-Religious. It is indeed the spiritual philosophies of human lives. Hence, Christianity not based on and emanating from the gospel is no Christianity at all.

About the Book

Christianity: The End of Spiritual Confusion is definitely a tapestry of inconvenient truth that unlocks the hidden mystery of Christianity. It biblically brings the almost forgotten, often relegated Christian Covenant out to the forefront of the reader's mind. It helps the reader fully understand the confusion that currently exists within the faith.

This book challenges its reader to examine many false beliefs, erroneous teachings and practices in the faith such as (1) the false belief that an angel whose name is Jehovah is God Almighty and (2) the false practice of paying tithes instead of giving. It makes a compelling case for the gospel explaining, in context, Jesus Christ, as the only author and finisher of the Christian faith. It positions its reader to probe the accounts that look into the manner of spirit that people who make headline news are operating in given our contemporary society today. On this premise, the author makes the bold move to introduce his ground-breaking 'Psychodynamics' theory of human behavior as well as his C-rule concept. Going beyond any controversy, this book biblically answers the existential question surrounding the chosen, beloved Jewish people on the face of the earth from the Christian perspective. It is indeed a life-line for a reader who loves to investigate the truth that makes one free, while living his or her everyday life.

Author's Biography

The Author, Bishop Lloyd Nsek, Sr., is a Nigerian-born American citizen with over 20 years of Christian ministry experience at the Pastoral level in Southern California. His confidence and critical thinking skills are God-given traits handed down from both his father (Engineer U. E. U. Nsek, a UCLA graduate) and his mother (Mrs. Nseyen Nsek, a Woodbury University graduate) respectively. Although his educational background in Business Management makes him a Phoenix, the author invariably finds his Christian calling highly irresistible.

Bishop Lloyd has a gigantic heart for the person of Jesus Christ. He is married to his lovely wife Josephine Nsek (a graduate of Moorhead State University) and they have four children. His ministry affiliations include Prayer of Faith Ministry Worldwide and The Lighthouse of Prayer Ministry.

He is currently a facilitator of one of the Small Groups Ministry at the seven-thousand plus members Water of Life Community Church in Fontana, California. Bishop Lloyd is now on seat with his mantle and mandate to begin the clean–up process of the filthiness of flesh and spirit in God's living temples—me and you.

www.ingramcontent.com/pod-product-compliance
Lightning Source LLC
Chambersburg PA
CBHW071540011025
33425CB00012B/703